MOTHERHOOD

MOTHERHOOD
An Experience in the Ghanaian Context

ELIZABETH R. TETTEY
Managing Director, ERAT Services, Accra, Ghana

GHANA UNIVERSITIES PRESS
ACCRA
2002

Published by
Ghana Universities Press
P. O. Box GP 4219
Accra, Ghana

Distributed in Europe and North America by African Books Collective
The Jam Factory, 27 Park End Street, Oxford OX1 IHU, UK
Email: abc@dial.pipex.com
Website: www.africanbookscollective.com

© Elizabeth R. Tettey, 2002
ISBN: 9964-3-0280-0

PRODUCED IN GHANA
Typeset by Ghana Universities Press, Accra, Ghana
Printed by SuperTrade Printing Press, Accra

To

My children: Karl, Winston and Isabella

and to

My nieces: Rose, Doris and Stella

CONTENTS

Preface	vii
Acknowledgements	xi

Chapter
1. THE SIGNIFICANCE OF THE MALE-FEMALE
   RELATIONSHIP — 1
   - The Origin of Mankind — 1
   - Child Reproduction — 1
   - Fertilization, Development of Embryo and Birth — 5
   - Child Personality — 9
   - Courtship — 11
   - The Mysteries of the Sexual Relationship — 12
   - Developmental Changes in the Girl-Child — 16

2. PREPARING GIRLS FOR ADULT ROLES — 17
   - Providing the Material Needs — 17
   - Help in the Girl's Choice of Her Life Partner — 20
   - The Role of the Spouse — 22
   - The Role of the Family — 23

3. THE CAREER OR WORKING WOMAN — 29
   - Formal Education of the Girl-Child — 29
   - Different Working Mothers — 30
   - Women Specialized Groups — 34
   - Greater Participation of Women — 37
   - Towards the Improvements of Problems of Women — 44

4. RIGHTS CONCERNING MARRIAGE, DIVORCE
   AND PROPERTY OWNERSHIP FOR WOMEN IN
   GHANA — 48
   - Forms of Marriage — 48
   - Marriage under the Ordinance — 49
   - Marriage under Mohammedans Ordinance (Cap 129) — 51
   - Rights in Marriage — 52
   - Rights in Divorce — 57
   - The Intestate Succession Law, 1985 — 59

5.	**CONCLUDING REMARKS**	62
	Perculiarities of Motherhood	62
	Instutionalizing Attitudes and Concerns of Motherhood	65
	Some Lessons drawn from the Scriptures	68

Bibliography   71

Index   73

PREFACE

There is often a conflict in the perception of motherhood and womanhood. As to whether motherhood is the fulfilment of womanhood or whether womanhood fulfils motherhood is debatable and still presents the chicken-and-egg type of scenario. Both have quite a complex and contradictory relationship. Ideally, a female should reach womanhood before getting married and before becoming a mother. Motherhood is often regarded as a more natural role but there are great differences in the meaning of motherhood from one society to the other. There are differences in ideas about conception, birth and childrearing, and in the relationship between mothers and their children particularly the extent to which mothers are solely responsible for the care of their own offspring.

Most women aspire to be mothers under patriarchy where they enjoy an imaginary status. Failure to achieve that imaginary status can be disappointing, even though patriarchy in itself is oppressive, subordinating and intimidating. The process of giving birth to children and caring for them, as a prerequisite to womanhood, changes women's sense of themselves, values and beliefs.

Most Ghanaian societies exhibit strong pro-natalist tendencies. The mother of many children is more highly regarded while the infertile woman is stigmatized and may go to any lengths to have a child. Such a stigmatized woman usually become a foster mother of children of her close relations, brothers, sisters or uncles.

Sometimes, women experience a rise or a fall when they become mothers. The rise or fall experience can be internal or external to the mother. A woman experiences a rise internally as a mother when the child she has carefully delivered, through the right choice of her spouse, appears with all the organs well represented, the child is active, shows a sign of intelligence and has a great resemblance to her or to her spouse. She feels fulfilled in the way that God showed satisfaction at creating all that He created on earth. This inward satisfaction as well as a sense of fulfillment urges her on to feel responsible for caring for the children.

Again, she experiences a rise in status if she has the strength to satisfy the needs of the children both materially and emotionally. Sometimes, however, even the initial transition to motherhood and the experience of motherhood in itself become a 'shock' to mothers when their expectations are not met. It could be that, the new child came with physiological or anatomical malformations, or that the mother does not have the financial means to cater for the children even at birth, or that a father rejects the child because of the circumstances surrounding the pregnancy. For the same reason, a woman after giving birth to a child may experience rejection not only from her spouse but also from other immediate family members and friends. These physical, social, economic and psychological inadequacies could be very upsetting and depressive and the mother will feel fallen because her expectations have not been met. The latter experience is external to the mother's inner feelings but can override and have a positive or a negative impact on how she experiences motherhood.

Motherhood brings new and enhanced authority to the mother within the home. A mother is responsible for most day-to-day decision-making about the child's care, health, socialization and education, although cultural norms dictate the scope and boundaries of this authority. In different cultures and in different homes, these authorities could be shared between the parents, or may be delegated to house supports such as aunties or uncles and, where working mothers are concerned, to even househelps such as housegirls or houseboys, nurses or nannies.

Becoming a mother is an astonishing event and is very important in the lives of most women. The relationship between mother and child is uniquely different to all others.

Motherhood has been described as every woman's true destiny, her primary goal in life and her sole means of achieving fulfillment as a human being when the children they bear are wanted and neither become juvenile deliquents nor adult vagabonds. Motherhood is a colossal role of a woman: her childbearing function and ability to provide nourishment for children through her own body must be far more fulfilling than her contribution, for example, to farming.

The world population census recorded 5.4 billion people in 1991 and of these 2.63 billion are females and 1.3 billion of the female population are mothers with as many children as twelve whilst others bear only one.

In some cultures, where the wife cannot bear a child the bondservant or niece takes her place in bed in order to ensure heirs. This is a practice that still exists among Moroccan Berbers in the middle of the Atlas Mountains where women marry a succession of men in order to provide legitimate heirs. It is similar to what Jacob did in the Old Testament when after paying a bride price in the form of years of labour for his bride Rachel, he had to take his bondservant to bed to give him an heir because Rachel could not bear him a child.

Motherhood is an important path to social status and personal achievement. Children are widely regarded as a great gift and blessing: they continue the family line and preserve property and wealth. They fulfil parents' needs for emotional support and companionship. Children can offer considerable emotional support to their mothers.

Motherhood is experienced under a wide range of conditions: economic, social and religious concepts and attitudes with variations from community to community and from one family to the other. Experiencing a fall or a rise in motherhood should be seen in the quality of children produced with regards to stature, intelligence, beauty and character and not whether the child was brought up in a farming community or, in the slum areas of a city or in the residential areas of the city or even in a hotel environment, or to rich or poor parents. The influences that these factors have on the quality of the child vary at large on the peace, love and harmony that exist at home between the parents.

This book discusses various aspects of motherhood in order to establish the possible ways by which and circumstances under which a child is conceived, born and bred. In my opinion, it is relative judgement to say a birth is a fallen case without knowing the vision of the mother or the parents, their culture and religious convictions, their readiness to nurture that seed to adulthood by their cultural and religious capabilities. I leave the reader to make his/her judgements as to what is a fall or a rise in motherhood.

Accra, October 2000 *Elizabeth R. Tettey*

ACKNOWLEDGEMENTS

I wish to thank the Lord God Almighty for the strength and courage which He has given me to write this book. It took a lot of effort to assemble the necessary information needed for documentation. Without His grace, I might not have succeeded.

I also wish to thank my church, Accra Ridge Church, as well as concerned friends and relatives for the spiritual support given to me.

I extend my special thanks to Mrs. Akua Kuenyehia for making some relevant documents available to me and to Rev. Dr S. Ayete-Nyampong and Mrs. Lilian Ayete-Nyampong for their valuable time and contributions in various forms for this book.

Many thanks go to Regina, my secretary, for typing out the script and for putting the script on diskettes for printing, and to the publisher for the production and publishing of the book.

Finally, I wish to express my responsibility for errors of any form that the reader may encounter in this book.

Chapter 1

THE SIGNIFICANCE OF THE MALE-FEMALE RELATIONSHIP

The Origin of Mankind

The origin of mankind can be traced through two schools of thought and remains debatable. There are the theological school and the scientific/genetic school of thought. The question, where do we come from is not answered when we mention our towns or villages or countries. There is a deeper origin, which is peculiar to every being. We need to explore how we are made.

Biblical studies on the creation teach how God created the first human beings, male and female, in his own image on the sixth day of the creation of the world and charging them to be in charge of all that He had created earlier, namely, Light and Darkness, Sky, Earth and Sea, Plants, Day and Night, other living beings, birds and animals — domestic and wild, large and small.

It is significant to note that whenever He created a life, whether animal or human, He blessed them. He charged them to reproduce so as to increase in number. It is significant also to note that he made both males and females. He made the man, according to the Bible, from the soil (Genesis 2: 7) and the woman, from the ribs of the man while He caused the man to fall into a deep sleep (Genesis 2: 21–22), and that forms the basis on which a man leaves his father and mother and becomes one with his wife. (Genesis 2:24).

The scientific/genetic school of thought postulates that mankind originates through a process of evolution of species from a lower to higher form over millions of years. Man finally emerges from this evolution by another process of scientific selection of species.

Scientifically, a man and a woman must be united in a sexual intercourse, in order to produce a child.

Child Reproduction

A sexual intercourse or mating at a favourable period, that is during ovulation period (fourteen days to the next menstrual period and within 36–72 hours of ovulation), produces a foetus which develops into a child. This is because the ovum i.e. the female sex cell (gamete), lives only up to 36–72 hours after which it dies.

Usually, the male gamete (sex cell) contributes XY chromosomes while the female gamete contributes XX chromosomes (Nyavor and Seddoh 1991). The male gametes are said to be heterogametic because they are of the X and Y type. The longer one is exactly like the X chromosome in females and the shorter one is the Y. Males, therefore, can contribute either an X or Y type of gamete. Each cell in the human body contains 23 pairs of chromosomes located in the nucleus, It is the 23rd pair which is the sex chromosome that determines the sex of the individual.

Unlike the male gamete, the female sex chromosomes are homogametic — they are double X (XX) and they produce only one type of gamete.

During fertilization, fusion of the sperm and egg occurs. An XY combination produces a male child while an XX combination produces a female child. Thus, sex of a child is determined at fertilization but ensuring which type of the male gamete fuses with the female gamete can help predetermine the sex of a child.

Under normal conditions, both the XX and XY zygotes have a 1:1 chance (Nyavor and Seddoh 1991). Possibilities of either a girl or a boy have mostly been by chance particularly because humans have only few children. Today, there is good news to learn that parents can select the sex of the children they want to bear by identifying the sex of the existing embryo and allowing the foetus to develop to term or terminate the pregnancy through artificially-accepted ways.

There are two ways by which the sex of the foetus is determined.

1. By amniocentesis, a test of the fluid around the embryo in the sixth week of pregnancy is done.

2. By a less reliable method of screening of an IVF embryo prior to its entry or implantation in the woman's body.

Aborting the unwanted embryo or implanting the desired one produces the desired sex. These selection methods are in use in Britain (Hanmer 1993). In India, amniocentesis followed by abortion is widely practised to select sons, instead of daughters for social reasons (Kishwar 1993).

There are other potential interventions which need to be considered for adoption. These include:

1   Those in use but not approved in UK:

1.1 Development of transgenic species from the mixture of genetic materials of different species including that of humans and other animal life.

1.2 Cloning which involves splitting the early embryo into separate cells to develop genetically identical individuals.

These are currently in use for the development of quality meat-producing male calves for beef herds and high-milk-producing female calves for dairy.

2. Those techniques yet to be developed include:

2.1 The determination of sex prior to fertilization — this is based on the scientific fact discussed earlier that the sperm determines the sex of the foetus because it has both the X and Y chromosomes. Identifying the X or Y-carrying sperm will, therefore, help to encourage the fertilization by the desired sperm and hence the sex of the foetus.

2.2 Ectogenesis which involves the conception and pregnancy outside a woman's body in an artificial womb.

2.3 Genetic counselling of adults and diagnosis of embryos — defective chromosomes and genes are identified and assessed and either selected or rejected based on the eugenic principle of reproducing genetically 'desirable' traits or individuals.

The possibilities for genetic manipulation of embryos are increasing and form a very serious area of study — a study of the chemical composition of say over 100,000 genes that each individual is made of (Hanmer 1993).

Today, there are various interventions to either prevent child reproduction or to enhance it. Some of these are listed.

Interventions to Prevent Child Reproduction

1. There are hormonal interventions as well as intra- uterine contraceptive devices (IUCDs) — barrier methods such as the use of diaphragm and condoms which a woman can adopt to prevent a pregnancy she is not both emotionally and financially prepared for.

Most of the family planning clinics offer counselling on these procedures either for a nominal fee or for nothing to the general public. Other contraceptive methods are sterilization — tubal ligation or vasectomy, and abstinence — avoidance of sexual intercourse when a woman wants to avoid pregnancy.

2. Coitus interruptus — withdrawal of the penis from the vagina before ejaculation.

3. Rhythm method — having sexual intercourse during safe periods only.

4. Use of contraceptive pills (hormonal tablets).

5. Use of spermicidal cream applied into the vagina before sexual intercourse kills the sperms on release and, therefore, prevents pregnancy.

6. Use of foaming tablets inserted into the vagina before sexual intercourse kills the sperms on release.

Interventions to Enhance Reproduction

There are also a number of services using hormonal products to increase conception. The UK Report on Human Fertilization and Embryology (Warnock Report 1993) outlined a number of services among which are:

1. Insemination by a donor (AID) which involves the introduction of sperm into the uterus of a woman.

2. *In vitro* fertilization (IVF) which involves the administration of hormones to induce superovulation producing more than one egg. Then, the removal of the ova surgically and fertilizing the ova in the laboratory and reimplanting in the woman.

3. Egg or embryo transfer which involves the removal of egg or embryo from one woman and implanting it in another woman.

4. Egg, sperm and embryo freezing.

5. Embryo flushing or lavage — a process of washing out fertilized

egg/embryo from one woman for study or for implantation in another woman.

6. Embryo experimentation which uses 'spare' embryos for research.

7. Surrogacy by which a woman by contract agrees to have or produce a child for someone. It could be done either by AID or by IVF or she may use her own eggs or those of another woman (Hanmer 1993).

Artificial insemination is the most unproblematic for women's health provided the sperm is not infected with HIV (Hanmer 1993). Other methods such as hormonal stimulation and surgical intervention involve both immediate and long-term health risks to the woman and/or her embryo.

Fertilization, Development of Embryo and Birth

This text will dwell mainly on how fertilization through sexual intercourse occurs.

During copulation, the male releases about 3–5 cubic millilitres of semen into the female vagina. In a normal circumstance, every cubic millilitre of semen contains 75–100 millions of spermatozoa. The sperms swim through the neck of the womb into the fallopian tubes. Millions of sperms may come into contact with the expelled ovum in the ampullary portion of the tube but usually only one succeeds in penetrating the membrane (Nyavor and Seddoh 1991). As soon as the head portion of the sperm enters the ovum, the tail is left behind. The successful fusion of the ovum and the head of the sperm is called fertilization which usually takes place in the widest portion of the fallopian tube. The two united cell structure is called the zygote. The zygote divides into four, then eight, doubling at every stage by a process called mitosis; also known as cleavage. It is propelled by ciliated lining of the fallopian tube into the womb. The journey takes about four days. By the time the developing human gets into the womb it is at a stage called morula — a ball-shaped structure.

If the male supplies the X sex decider, the developing baby will be a girl. If the father gives off the Y sex decider, the result will be a baby boy. So if a couple is having only girls, the man should not blame the woman. It is he who will be giving off the Y sex decider to produce XY instead of an XX zygote. Sometimes, however, the vaginal fluid is capable of destroying the Y chromosome so that only the X survives with resultant girl babies.

It is worth noting here that once the man has given off the sperm which gets fully matured only after fertilization, he can live on the moon and the baby will be developed to full term if the woman, that is the mother's constitution, and the womb are healthy. Apart from the need for a healthy woman to start pregnancy, she needs to be protected from many risks which can kill her.

Some of these risks are: excessive bleeding if she miscarries; profound bleeding in case of ectopic pregnancy, that is, pregnancy outside the normal site; a disease peculiar to pregnant women only called pregnancy-induced-hypertension. Others include excessive bleeding before the baby is due, soon after delivery or days after delivery; infection as a result of low quantity and quality of blood that is, anaemia or poor care during the process of delivery or after delivery. All these risks can kill the woman. This kind of death is termed maternal death or mortality. It is so high in developing countries including Ghana. It is perhaps for these risks that the presence of the man is needed for his timely intervention and assistance to health clinics.

Hormones — oestrogen and progesterone produced by the ovary continue to maintain development in the uterus and also stop all follicles from developing and thereby preventing further ovulation and menstruation. After three months of pregnancy, the corpus luteum (the space left in the ovary after the expulsion of the ovum or sex cell) degenerates and a structure, the placenta, is formed to take over the secretion of hormones of the corpus luteum. The placenta is made up of numerous root-like structures called villi which are highly vascularized. The placenta is connected to the body of the embryo by a long cord-like structure called the umbilical cord. The artery transports food and oxygenated blood from the embryo while the vein transports waste metabolic products and deoxygenated blood from the embryo to the placenta (Nyavor and Seddoh 1991). The villi form a barrier between the blood of the mother and that of the baby. This means that if there is no abnormality the mother's blood does not come into direct contact with that of the baby. It is, therefore, not correct to imagine that by the seventh month of pregnancy, the baby is in a pool of blood so he/she cannot survive if he/she is born at that period. (This is an Akan perception).

In fact, by the sixth week of pregnancy, the baby's heart is already functioning. The heart beats can be picked by a machine called Sonicaid, loud enough for by-standers to hear the beats. Again it is wrong to perceive that at six to eight weeks, the developing baby is a blood clot and so can be aborted without remorse..The head and facial features and external sex organs are developed and all major organs are laid down in their primitive form (Fig. 1)

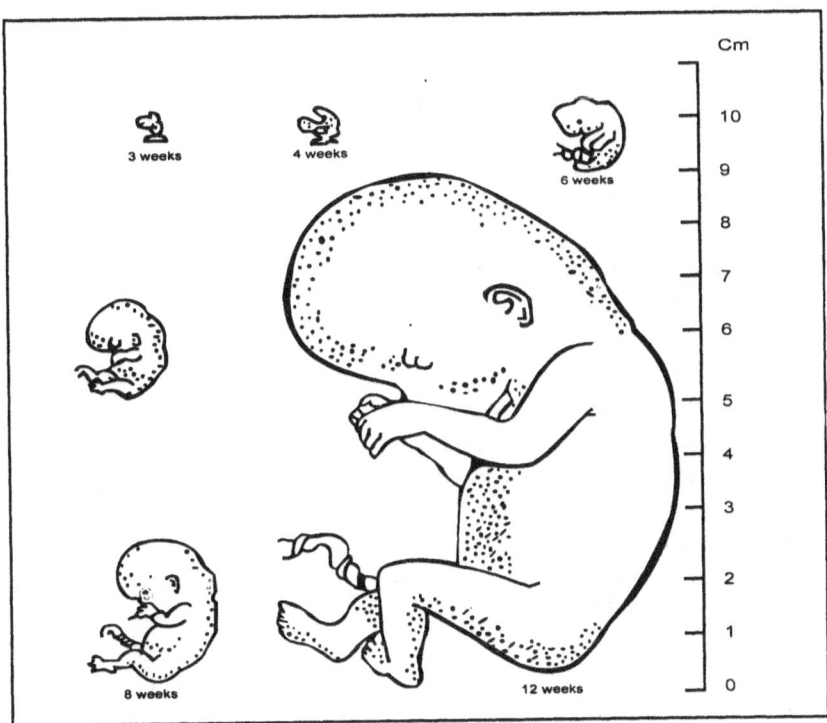

Fig. 1: Size of embryo between 3 and 12 weeks of pregnancy.

Source: Myles Margaret F. 1985. *Textbook for Midwives with Modern Concepts of Obstetric and National care* (10th Edn), Churchill Livingstone, Edinburgh by kind permission of the publisher.

The embryo is enclosed in four embryonic membranes, namely, chorion, amnion, allantois and the yolk sac. The outer membrane, the chorion, encloses and protects the other membranes as well as the embryo and portions help form the placenta which, by the end of the twelve weeks of pregnancy, takes over the nourishment and excretion of the foetus almost completely. Before the twelfth week, the embryo is nourished through processes maintained by the female hormones — progesterone and oestrogen produced by the corpus luteum. The corpus luteum continues to produce diminished amounts of progesterone and oestrogen until the twentieth week of pregnancy when the placenta takes over completely. The amnion is a sac containing liquid, the amniotic fluid, which provides a watery environment in which the embryo develops. This fluid is also 'a shock absorber' for the embryo. The allantois and yolk sac do not feature significantly in the development of the foetus.

The blood circulatory systems of the mother and embryo are not in direct contact but selective exchanges of material from one to the other occur here. Food substances and oxygen diffuse from the mother into the embryo while waste metabolic substances of carbon dioxide diffuse from the embryo into the mother (Nyavor and Seddoh 1991).

The gestation period of the embryo is usually 40 weeks (Fig. 1). By 12 weeks, the baby is fully formed and the expectant mother begins to be aware of its presence from having sharp "kicks". This is an exciting period during which the husband can be made aware of what is happening in the womb and be made to share the joy in expecting. After 40 weeks, the thick wall of the uterus undergoes regular powerful contractions (labour). The abdominal wall also contracts and eventually the embryonic membranes are broken. The amniotic fluid flows out through the vagina and by so doing lubricates the birth canal. The cervix dilates as well as the vagina, which is now highly thickened and muscular. The foetus with its head lying towards the cervix, gradually emerges through the vagina and the baby is born.

The portion of the cord on the baby is tied with thread in two places and then cut between the tied areas to prevent bleeding. It dries up gradually and falls off leaving a scar on the baby called the navel, which is, always there on all humans be they female or male. Some people have ball-type navels, others have hidden navels. The remaining portion of the umbilical cord, the placenta and the embryonic membranes in the mother are forced out by contractions of the abdominal and uterine walls. These are collectively known as the "afterbirth". The "afterbirth" must be expelled necessarily to prevent them from decaying within the mother and causing blood poisoning. In the olden days, lots of mothers lost their lives through the retention of the "afterbirth" (Nyavor and Seddoh 1991).

Sometimes, both ovaries may release ova simultaneously. If ova from two ovaries are fertilized at the same time fraternal twins are produced and they may be of the same sex or different sexes. If a fertilized egg divides into two and develops into two separate embryos, genetically identical twins are produced. When there is a problem with the division of the fertilized egg, Siamese twins are produced. The resulting children are joined together and may share some of the vital organs. In some cases, it is possible to save one or both children through surgery.

If for one reason or the other, couples are unable to produce children it may be due to low sperm-count in the man or blocked oviducts in the woman. Often fertility drugs are recommended to stimulate the ovaries to release the ova. These drugs can, however, stimulate the release of too many ova and multiple fertilization occurs resulting in the birth of polypoids—twins, triplets or others (Nyavor and Seddoh 1991).

Thus, to give birth, the woman must give off similar number of chromosomes as the man in order for a human being to be formed. She has the extra responsibility of harbouring the baby in her womb to nourish him/her for up to 40 weeks, of labouring for at least 15–24 hours and going through a hard push to bring forth a human being at a very high risk of her life. Every human being owes his/her mother a great deal of gratitude. In fact, women need to be cherished. For, even after the nine months of risk period, the mother is required by the World Health Organization to feed the baby solely on her body fluid, breast milk, for six whole months.

Child Personality

Having discussed the possible genetic contributions that the sex chromosomes can make, we shall focus the following discussion on the personality of the child. The personality of the child begins to be influenced by certain traits inherited through either the X and Y chromosomes. Unfortunately, certain diseases such as asthma, diabetes mellitus can be passed on to the child genetically.

The child's looks, actions, thinking and behaviour altogether go to make up his/her personality. Personality is also influenced by the environment in which the child grows. The environment could be the totality of her home, family, school, friends, religion and community. Thus, the effect or influence of these factors yields a child of a personality, said to be kind, pleasant, respectful, honest, confident and so on.

With regard to girls, puberty or adulthood begins usually at the age 14 on the average. Today, we have cases when girls even begin to menstruate at the age of 8. Depending on nutritional levels and other environmental practices, puberty could be earlier or later. As soon as the girl is able to ovulate i.e. up to two years after the first menses, she is in a state that can receive the male sperm and effect fertilization and become a mother. However, in rare cases, she may not necessarily be prepared emotionally, mentally and physically to go through motherhood.

The girl at puberty would need to be economically sound to think of becoming a mother. She must be prepared economically to provide all the things her baby will need and all that she as mother will need. Ideally, this means she will, as in most cases, be ready only after she has completed her education and hopefully, acquired a profession. She could then be gainfully employed and be assured of a regular income which will cater for her baby, herself and her spouse. In short, she must be ready to acquire and maintain a home either single-handedly or with the help of a spouse. In rare cases, if she chooses to be a single – parent, she could be assisted by her parents.

Thus, at this stage a girl at puberty begins to have a vision of the kind of family she wants to establish. Will it be an ideal, happy, well-united family built on Christian principles and ideals if she comes from a Christian family or if she is a Christian by herself. If she is a Moslem, she will definitely have a vision that will enhance the religious ideologies of a Moslem.

When her vision or goals are set, she has to look at the necessary tools or thrusts she has to enable her to achieve or realize her goals. She will need to examine what human resources she needs apart from her spouse to enable her to achieve her vision. She will need to understand and explore what rights she has legally, religiously and culturally to enable her to realize this vision. Her vision must be revised periodically and not be stagnant since the thrusts she needs to achieve these goals can be environmentally influenced or directed.

She decides in consultation with her future partner, how many children she would want to have, what kind of education she would want to provide her children. She must also have a vision of a good job which will facilitate excellent child-care and a liberal husband. This means that her husband would be loving and caring and will stand firm by her in her trial moments particularly during her child bearing years for the attainment of their vision.

A serious interaction with her siblings and in-laws, and close and supportive friends could yield fruitful results towards their vision.

Sometimes, a girl could be careless and childish in the choice of the kind of future partner she sets out for. In her youth, with an unassuming mind all her peers are potential future partners. Parental guide on the dangers of selecting one partner to the other is essential since she may be blind to see even the most glaring of the factors that go against her choice. She could also suffer a loss from disappointment from a loved one or from objections from her parents or parents of a loved one.

In all these cases, she must be firm on what to look out for because she would be led to her second best choice, God being her help and guide. When the choice is made, she must settle with whoever becomes her partner and use the available thrusts to make the partnership fruitful.

The economic, social and emotional preparations needed by girls apply to boys as well. In most patriarchal societies, a more economic and emotional stability is expected of the boys as prospective fathers. The boys provide most of the assurances that the couple needs as future parents. This notion could hold where most of a woman's contribution in the home had not been quantified and documented.

Courtship

The Bible teaches us that our Lord Jesus Christ was conceived by the Holy Spirit (Matthew 1: 20). However, all humans result from a union between the male and female — man and woman.

A woman needs to have a broad mind about sex and must be psychologically prepared against all odds because she is biologically disadvantaged: she goes through menstrual cycles with its discomforts and rules to "safe" sex periods; she has a limited child-bearing period in her lifetime and she goes through menopausal stages with all its inconveniences and demands. She must work out a normal relationship with a partner and plan when she wants to be a mother as guided today by the existence of the many programmes of health workers and the Planned Parenthood Associations, marriage counsellors of the various churches and most importantly through the church leaders and priests.

In the non-Christian life, courtship means that there must be a union between a female and a male. This is achievable most commonly through a sexual intercourse or artificially through the other artificial interventions mentioned earlier on in this Chapter.

The union through a sexual intercourse is usually a delicate union and normally cannot be instant. It has to be cultured and nurtured to happen. It is universal and unchanging; something that is the biological make-up of each individual. There is usually a period of courtship. The girl and her male partner get to know each other through discussions and sharing ideas together on matters related to their environment, profession or religion. They are more likely to develop such an intimacy when they share common views on a number of issues.

However, in rare and under unpleasant situations, the girl could be sexually abused resulting even in pregnancy. Rape, as violence against women. is discussed later in this book. Such an abuse could lead to a number of emotional disturbances throughout the life of the girl. At times, girls experience violence and ill-treatments because, to such rapists, it is the best way to educate innocent girls about sex. There are various reasons and forms of rape which are not discussed here.

There are provisions under the law to protect the girl against all forms of sexual abuse provided such incidents are reported to the right authorities who are custodians of the right of the girl-child.

A baby could be born either through a normal courtship and consent between parents either in marriage or through an extra-marital relationship or through rape. Perhaps after an experience of a rape, a woman can consent to a normal relationship with her boyfriend or husband to enable her to overcome the ill effects of a rape on her emotions.

Whichever way it happens, the girl-child must be prepared to protect herself and her child and be able to provide her needs and that of the child. If she is unable to meet all these odds, she suffers all kinds of discomforts, frustrations that can be very stressful.

It is worth noting that both Christianity and Islam abhor premarital sex.

The Mysteries of the Sexual Relationship

Human beings like other mammals are unisexual. The reproductive system is essentially a tract that leads from the gonads (ovaries and testes) to the outside in both males and females (Fig. 2). The male reproductive system consists of two testes, enclosed in a scrotal sac, epididymis, spermatic cord, a penis, vas deferens, urethra, seminal vesicle which carries the seminal fluid or semen which is passed via the urethra through the penis into the vagina during a sexual intercourse. The female has two oval ovaries attached to the body wall in the lower region of the abdominal cavity, one below each kidney (Nyavor and Seddoh 1991).

The testes have been placed outside the body because the body temperature is too high for optimum sperm production. The testes produce the hormone testosterone, male sex hormone which is responsible for the development of male secondary characteristics. They also manufacture spermatozoa or sperms which are male sex cells.

In the testes are found highly coiled-up structures called seminiferous

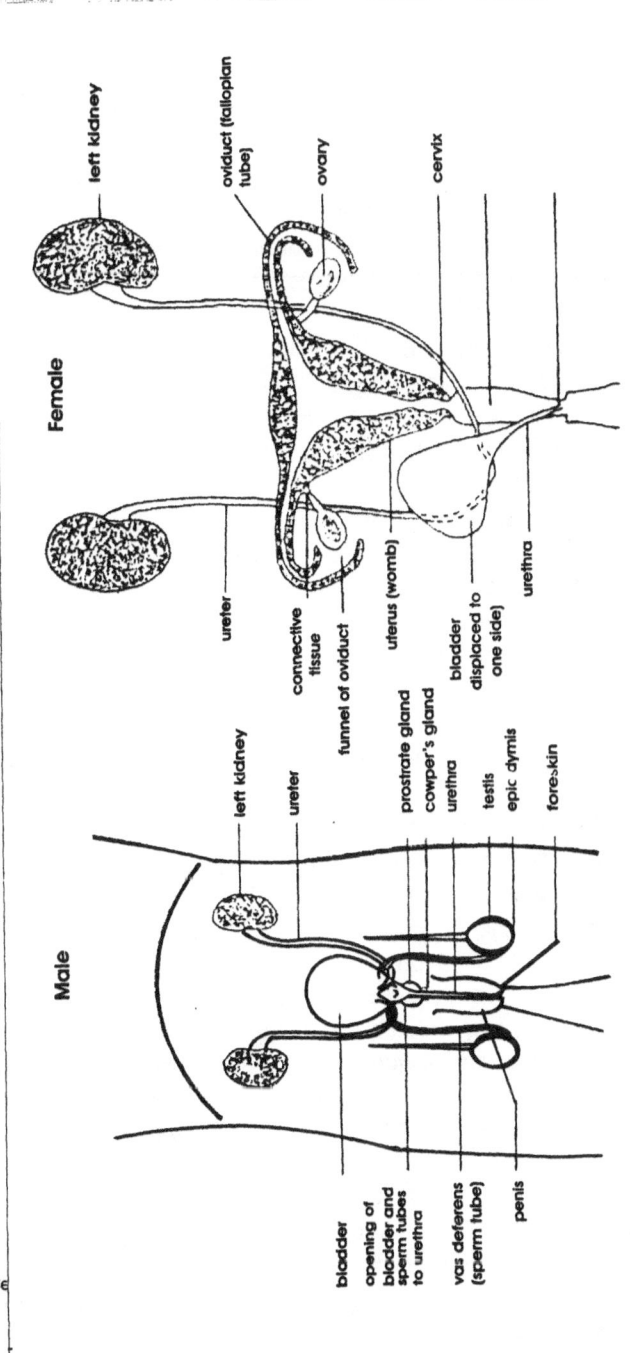

Fig. 2: The Reproductive system of the human male and female.
Source: After Fig.15.12 in Nyavor, C. B. and S. Seddoh 1991. *Biology for Senior Secondary Schools*. Unimax Publishers Limited in association with Macmillian Publishers Ltd., London and Basingstoke, by kind permission of the publishers.

tubules which unite to form larger coiled-up structures known as epididymis which mature the sperms and produce secretions for that purpose. To each epididymis is attached a sperm duct called the vas deferens through which pass two spermatic cords containing the spermatic artery and vein.

The cords continue the transportation process of sperms. The seminal vesicle which produces seminal fluid are found at the base of the urethra which is a long tube inside the penis. The prostrate gland also surround the base of the urethra. Just beneath the prostrate glands are the cowper's glands, the ejaculatory duct.

All four structures immediately mentioned above open into the urethra; which is long and passes through the penis to open at the tip. The urethra performs the functions of urination and transportation of spermatozoa with the seminal fluid into the female during sex act. It is, therefore, known as genito-urinary tube.

The human penis is made up of a spongy tissue and highly vascularized muscles. The spongy tissue contains spaces, which become filled with blood during sexual excitement. This makes the penis erect so that it may be placed in the female. The end of the penis is covered and protected by a loose retractable skin called the foreskin. (Nyavor and Seddoh 1991). The foreskin is usually removed in the process of circumcision.

The ovaries produce eggs or ova and female sex hormones (oestrogen and progesterone) which control the development of female secondary characteristics. The hormones also initiate the thickening of the wall of the uterus in readiness for implantation of the fertilized egg. The fallopian funnel lying close to each ovary conducts the discharged egg from the ovary through the fallopian tube into the uterus. The muscular neck of the uterus, the cervix, projects into the vagina. In the female, the vagina remains separate from the urethra (a passage for urine).

The vaginal orifice is guarded by inner and outer lips (labia minora and labia majora respectively) which open into the vulva. Lying in front of the vulva is a small, sensitive organ called the clitoris which contains an erectile tissue (Nyavor and Seddoh 1991). Heat periods in the female i.e. periods when she is ready to engage in copulation with the male occur every 28 days on the average. One egg is released alternatively by the two ovaries in a process known as ovulation. Occasionally, two eggs are released at a time by each ovary (which could lead to unidentical twins). The ovum, by a ciliary action gets swept into the fallopian tube where it may become fertilized if it meets a sperm. The corpus luteum produces progesterone, a hormone which causes thickening of the walls of the uterus in readiness to receive a fertilized ovum for implantation. If there is no implantation, the thick lining of the uterine wall breaks down. The breakdown substances of the uterine wall and the unfertilized egg are discharged with a quantity of blood from the vagina. This process is known as menstruation and occurs in a menstrual cycle, usually every 28 days, under normal circumstances.

At this time, some girls develop or experience uncomfortable situations, such as lower abdominal pains, lower back pains and painful thighs referred to as dysmenorrhoea and some experience vomiting and headaches called premenstrual syndrome. In such states, they often have to report to the clinic for treatment to control their state. Sometimes, they are put on painkillers such as paracetamol and brufen or recommended to lay their abdomen on hot-water bottles to ease the flow of blood and to alleviate their pain. Both the girl and the parents receive counselling to manage the situation.

At this period, it is important for the girl/woman to observe very strict personal hygiene. She needs to have her bath regularly at least twice a day. In acute profuse blood flow cases, she may need a bath three times a day and must report this abnormality to a gynaecologist. Disposable feminine pads are used to receive the blood loss. In the rural areas, where feminine pads are not known, or cannot be afforded, strips of cloth are used. In some very traditional societies, the woman has to be seated on a hole for the five days of the menstrual period to release the blood. She is considered unclean for this period and barred from entering some holy places of the kings, and the home of fetish priests in the village or township — a common practice in some villages in the Volta Region of Ghana. Modern societies have no policies on girls during their menstrual periods. Christian ladies can attend church and worship normally during menstrual period.

When God created man, he charged him to go and produce. (Genesis 1:28). Reproduction is necessarily effected through a process of fertilization. Fertilization can be effected only after copulation or sexual intercourse between man and woman. However, currently, fertilization can be made in the laboratory through the artificial processes discussed in this book such as *in vitro* fertilization. The union and its resultant foetus/child fulfils God's plan for mankind for the continuity of the human race and man should be respected for withstanding all odds to be made into man or woman. Even the resultant child from an artificial means requires that a male and a female gamete be brought together to fulfil the union.

Developmental Changes in the Girl-Child

The average weight of the child is 3.2 kilogrammes and ranges between 1.8 and 4.5 kilogrammes at birth. Weight gains are quicker in the girl-child than in the male child and by year 12; the girl-child reaches her adult height while the boy-child reaches his adult height by the age of 18. Some children grow fast in some years and slow down at other times. Development in girls is fastest between six years and twelve years. The rate of growth of each girl-child varies with genetic traits and the environmental factors.

At the adolescent stage, the girl-child moves into adulthood. Changes begin to show on the body and the adolescent child experiences a sexual growth at puberty, which for girls manifests between the ages of eleven and thirteen and for boys at the age of 13–14. Some of the visual changes include the development of the breasts, menstruation occurs, hairs begin to show at the armpit and around the sexual organ, the waist becomes defined and slim while the hips broaden. Like for boys, the glands that speed up growth become very active especially those that supply oil to the hair and skin and, therefore, many suffer from pimples, black heads and other skin rashes. As the adolescent grows physically, she also grows in the ways she thinks and understands. This mental development enables her to perform various duties assigned to her both at home and at school. She is able to solve problems and begins to ask intelligent questions. Socially, she slowly learns to walk in groups with her peers and plays together with them. She takes on both good and bad habits from these friends. They enjoy sporting activities together e.g. ampe, and scotch.

At this stage also, she begins to learn to choose between what is right and wrong. This means, she is beginning to make moral decisions from what she learns from people and conditions around her. She also begins to practice good health habits such as giving herself enough rest, feeding properly both adequately and timely, taking good care of her body—bathing and washing her dirty clothes and ironing them. She also engages herself in regular exercises. It is, therefore, obvious that at this stage her thinking, the way she talks, the way she dresses, the way she behaves towards others, her attitudes to right or wrong are results of the cultural, social and religious values of the community in which she develops. Again, this community attitude varies from place to place — be it a village, town or city. Variations in locality are influenced by the availability of social amenities such as schools, hospitals, markets, water and electricity.

Chapter 2

PREPARING GIRLS FOR ADULT ROLES

Providing the Material Needs

The ante-natal care for both males and females is the same. The care for multiple pregnancy — for twins whether they are both males, female and male or both females — is slightly different because the woman expecting twins or triplets or more will require more rest. In fact, she might have to be admitted into hospital around 30 weeks gestation to prevent premature birth. She will require extra food, extra iron and vitamin supplements. So her care is different from the mother with a singleton baby.

In Ghana, the educated and well-informed pregnant woman with the help of the husband, parents or relatives, boyfriend or friends from her church, begins to show concern for what she needs for the unborn child, right from the day the pregnancy test is recorded positive. The uneducated pregnant woman does not usually want or wish that her pregnancy is known to others until the stomach bulges out and would not even go for a pregnancy test until after three to five months. In the true Ghanaian culture, purchases for the unborn child is not the norm. It is the formally educated women who borrow this idea from the developed world.

When an enlightened woman thinks she has taken all the necessary precautions — gone through the customary, religious and ordinance processes of getting married or acquiring a spouse, the advent of pregnancy is a great excitement. With this excitement she begins to think of her needs as a pregnant woman and the needs of the unborn child. There is also the anticipation that at certain stages of the pregnancy she may not be in a healthy state to look for things she will need when she is in confinement.

The élite pregnant woman, therefore, makes purchases of the items which can be used for both sexes for the first few months. Such kit include; baby cot and carry cot, napkins, safety pins, cot sheets, blankets, buckets, feeding bottles and the accessories (these are being discouraged now), mackintosh, unisex dresses of white and yellow colours, for blue is reservedly for boys while pink is most universally used for girls. The toiletries of the child include, toilet soap, baby body creams and lotions, heat rash powder, dusting powder, zinc ointment, etc. There should also be a first aid kit of syrups ranging from paracetamol, multivitamins, anti-diarrhoea, to plasters, gauzes, cotton wool and gentian violet which will help heal minor cuts, sores and rashes. Then, as the child develops, the needs vary with the stage of development. Even teething powder must be available to alleviate teething pains as the baby develops the first set of teeth.

For comfort and also to keep the child from mischief, there must be a good number of toys ranging from walkers to colour identification toys. For an average-income woman, the above are basic provisions for children among urban and city dwellers. Mind you, in our rural settings, mere used-clothes, a special wash basin, some toilet soap, a towel and a few clothes are enough—it was under those conditions that you and I were born, if you are fifty years and above and born to mere peasant farmers.

The list in the developed world, definitely, is different. It is much longer. Browsing through the Internet, one sees a long list of needs for mothers and children. Diapering accessories go beyond napkins and include diaper bags, diaper pails liners, potty seats and wipe. For feeding, bottles, booster seats, breast pumps, food and formula, high chair in the bathroom, bath seats, bath tubs lotion and powder. For safety measures, special maternity pillow, and sleepers are needed during the period of the pregnancy. In the first three months to one year when the child is born, bouncer carriers, car seats, play pens, strollers cradles, cribs, bedding —mattress and blankets, bassinets, changing tables, furniture accessories, are provided.

At the early stages of development the child sometimes could share a bed with the mother, or lie in the cot beside the mother's bed or in a cot in a room near the mother's room. As the child grows up, a separate room may be provided.

Other needs that specifically are peculiar to the girl-child include the ear-ring of various designs and shapes, bracelet, necklace and shoe with a bag to match. Some very rich and exclusive parents provide matching hats even in remote villages in Ghana for a growing girl.

Gradually, the child grows up and gets into a primary school to begin formal education. Here, the major needs include the school uniform which is accepted at the particular school he/she gets enrolled into, a school bag of a design and size affordable by her parents, school shoes or casual shoes, sports wear, lunch box (which is an urban phenomenon) packed everyday with snacks (sandwich, buns, toast, with drinks, juices or water). Of course, the girl wears along the ear-rings of sizes permitted in her school (if at all).

Young children need a guide or a driver to take them to and from school. They need their parents, mostly the mother to be by them providing their meals and guiding them throughout what to do before and after school. She lays emphasis on 'do's 'and 'dont's ' relevant for their guide. In rural settings, some fifty years back, peasant parents provided typical breakfast ranging from gari and beans, *apapransa, koose, kenkey* and fish to as heavy meals as *konkonte* and palmnut soup made with cow hide ('welle') and *ampesi* i.e. boiled yam or plantain or cocoyam or cassava with stew or soup. In the urban and city areas, however, breakfast is usually beverages served with plain bread, toasted bread and eggs and porridge made from cereals.

Children must be presented in school uniforms well ironed and without folds. They need to have all their textbooks purchased well in time before the beginning of the school year. In cases where the child could not have these needs provided by the parents, he/she had to fall on other relations, aunts, uncles or even cousins either through the initiative of his/her parents or through his/her own initiative to enable the determined child to attend school. Even though our rural settings and culture, over the years, make us responsible for each other—being your brother's keeper-type of attitude, in recent times, it is a fall if one cannot look after children one bears. A child whose needs cannot be provided by her own parents is perceived as having problems—a fallen case.

At the secondary school or boarding school level, the needs of the child increases. Like other fellow students, the child is furnished with a long kit list to bring to school, for this marks the beginning of learning how to stay away from his parents' home and be on his own. Basically, therefore, the requirements of clothing include dresses and the formal Ghanaian dresses as allowed by the particular school. Beddings including mattresses, blankets and bedsheets, pillows and pillow cases must be provided. Other needs include shoes of everyday wear and sports wear, panties, vests and brassiers as relevant underwears for girls and panties, socks and singlets for boys.

Further, they must be provided with toiletries, body creams, powder and deodorants to keep their body from any form of smell and to give them an inviting fresh scent always.

Of course, if they have to go to a boarding school, children need agricultural tools such as cutlass and hoe. These days, they must also take along for each school term, a scrubbing brush in addition to a cutlass and a hoe. Normally, because of poverty in the rural settings, a child in a boarding school is highly admired by the village community particularly because most of such school children are obedient and respectful and keep themselves neat at a profile higher than they would have been if they were left in the rural settings to grow into adulthood. Such children begin to show maturity and begin to show independence.

At the tertiary school-level, most of the needs are as in the secondary school level. In addition, such adult students are provided with extra facilities such as portable stoves and cooking pans to enable the student to cook her own meals. Further, a radio, a refrigerator and fan, floor and wall decorations are provided to create a good surrounding to enhance studies.

After graduation, the girl immediately needs a good accommodation with basic facilities such as kitchen, bath and toilets. The girl will require, at least, a hard furnishing: a bed with mattress, dinning table and cooking facilities. The needs, as before, must be constantly replenished and maintained. The girl needs to be supported until she begins to live on her own and continues to supply her own needs.

Economic or material influences are only a means to an end and do not form the only influences on the education of the child. Thus, economic influences on schooling often conflict with other more important goals. It is, no doubt, a fact that economic processes and purposes do shape education, which prepares the child to become better equipped to introduce or effect changes in her own life and the life of others.

Help in the Girl's Choice of her Life Partner

As parents, we have the moral obligation to give equal opportunities to our children, be they girls or boys, physically, morally and economically.

In fulfilling the physical make up of our children, we have to be largely concerned in the choice of our life partners from whom these traits are passed on to our children. These traits are genetic materials (chromosomes) which carry the relevant information that enables humans to be the individuals that they are. Parental heights is the most obvious of these traits. Studies today have estimated the adult height of the child as the average of the height of the two parents, plus or minus 7 cm for boys and girls respectively (Stanhope and Jacob 1995).

Short stature in children can be very disturbing and can be mistaken to be Turner syndrome. Short stature is a main feature of Turner syndrome. In girls, this is detected at the age 2 or 3 years when growth begins to slow down. Medically, heights of children with defects like Turner syndrome are being improved by growth hormones such as oxandrolone, an anabolic steroid and oestrogen. Studies are still being conducted to determine the exact doses to use, the sequence and combination of treatment as well as the age at which such treatments could be started. These medications are available as tablets while other growth hormones could be given as injections daily subcutaneously (under the skin) (Stanhope and Fry 1995).

Thus, for a concern for the physical look or the stature of the unborn child, parents need to guide the girl and raise strong objections to the choice of her life partner. If the girl does not meet or succeed in making the right choice of the man, she will need to be directed and introduced to other means to achieve producing children of the average height, intelligence and beauty. It is in this instance that she necessarily has to use the services provided by the planned parenthood clinics, the marriage counsellors and seek for the commitment of her brothers, cousins, brother-in-laws and even close friends. These efforts must be supported with serious committed prayers and good dietary practices.

Beside the physical look of a spouse, parents are also concerned about the religious and cultural backgrounds of the spouse. Parents are more relaxed when there are similarities in these backgrounds. From their own experience, such couples would be compatible for their journey together as husband and wife. Parents may not be able to narrate all the experiences — failures or successes to their children for fear that it can have a negative influence on the child they want to jealously protect. Quite often, however, such experiences have hidden influences on helping to choose or accept a spouse for their child.

In some areas in Ghana, rigid cultural norms exist and couples find it difficult to make a breakthrough or inject modern social practices. For example, in the developed world, it is fun for the female (wife) to receive her breakfast tray from the husband while sleeping late in the morning but in some parts of Ghana, it is a taboo to see a man serving the wife. It must always be the other way round.

Also religious practices differ if the couple belong to different religions. One of them, and usually it must be the woman, who has to accept the religious practices of the man. Even in matrilineal homes, this attitude is not different. Some families believe and benefit in the saving Grace of the stripes of Jesus, others have difficulties to benefit from this Grace because of social attitudes and practices.

Parents, having assisted their children through school and equipped them with a profession must also help them settle down with the spouses chosen in the provision of adequate shelter. At this point, they direct the couple-to-be through the necessary engagement and marriage ceremonies to see them start life together as husband and wife.

Parental roles both shape and are shaped by the allocation of domestic and child-care responsibilities and the ways in which men and women relate to one another in their partnership. The behavioural and ideological practices of parents are also formed in a larger arena than simply the household. The discourses concerning child-care and childhood have required greater participation and new skills on the part of parents, notably, mothers.

The discourses surrounding motherhood have emphasized the centrality of the mother-child relationship. In some family set-ups, full-time maternal care was seen as essential in the prevention of emotional disorders in children and the maximization of children's potential through the achievement of 'normal' development. The main agent through whom the norms of child development are to be achieved is the mother; she is required not only to develop her child but also to take pleasure in doing it. Children could suffer a set-back in development if for one reason or the other the mother is under stress and is unable to offer her guide and counsel during their developmental stages.

Ideologies such as who wins the bread for the family, and love in the marriage tend to emphasize similarities within the couple and are central to the mother-child relationship.

The Role of the Spouse

Since we have discussed preparations of the girl-child our spouse here is mainly the husband or the selected lucky man. This man must have received all the merits on his stature and beauty, his educational level and profession already. As an aspiring spouse, his immediate needs include a shelter for his family.

He must have inherited the shelter from his parents or acquired through his workplace or arrange to acquire with his spouse through a mortgage loan. In the traditional system, a man aspiring to marry is required to be equipped with the necessary tools. As a farmer, he must have land, a cropped area, a place of abode; as a hunter he must have a gun and again, a place of abode. These requirements ensure that when he marries, he can provide shelter, clothing and food to the spouse and children.

Today, most young ladies are satisfied when the man is equipped with a university degree or a non-degree profession or a gainful employment. It is assumed he will be able in the very near future, to provide shelter, clothing and, food for his spouse and children. In lieu of the above, he needs to think over it with his fiancée for acquisition of rented apartment. It means he must be prepared to meet the monthly rental charges.

At present in Ghana, there are numerous estate-developers ready to help the young man or couple to acquire shelter of their own. Some of these developers include, the Regimanuel Gray Ltd., the Home Finance Company, CFC Estates, the Mansonian Green Developers among others. These developers also have various financial arrangements in place to assist the aspiring couple.

Having succeeded in securing shelter, the young man will need to equip the house with a hard or soft type furnishing depending on his income or the available provisions made by his employers and/or parents. The young man then needs to meet the cultural, religious and legal requirements to give effect to his marriage to his fiancée either with the help of his parents and/or relatives or even friends.

Essentially, the parents and/or relations set out to make investigations on the woman proposed by their son in the same way that parents and relatives of the woman do to ascertain their daugther's safety with the man's family with regard to hereditary diseases and criminal records in the family and also how respectable the man is himself. According to Dolphyne (1991), emotional attachments develop later and, therefore, love between a young man and a young woman is not in itself considered legitimate grounds for marriage.

Role of the Family

A Christian family requires that when a man marries he leaves his parents and become united with his wife and become one with her (Genesis 2: 24). The institution of marriage, among other things, is meant to prevent immorality in societies. Every woman must have a husband and every man a wife and each of them have duties or responsibilities to each other. Each of them have a hold on the other's body. They should not deny themselves to one another. If for some reason they have to deny each other, it is prudent that they resume access to each other at the earliest possible time. This is to avoid them being swayed away from each other by people of the opposite sex (1. Corinthians 7: 2–6). de Graft Johnson (1994) defines the family as a social institution which recruits members and ensures its continuity through marriage and procreation. The family applies blood relationship to determine members who are born into it and a principle of affinity through marriage to ensure a supportive kinship structure. The concept of the family is elastic and ranges from its simplest form of the nuclear family (husband, wife with or without children) to the extended family which embodies the lineage of direct descendants of an ancestor or ancestress through a male or female line. This concept is recognized in most African and specifically Ghanaian societies for land ownership, succession to traditional offices or property inheritance. The family is a mechanism for survival by ensuring the nurturing, caring, socialization, protection and material well-being of its members. By the same token, the family forms the basis of any society and nation and ensures a constant supply of new members or citizens (Ardayfio-Schandorf 1994: 14). Any changes or events which threaten the survival, stability, health and living standards of families also threatens the nation or state.

The functions of the family include, among other things, satisfying the perennial needs of human beings for food, clothing and shelter on one hand and sexual gratification, procreation and child-rearing on the other. Even though these needs can be attained outside the family, it is in the family that these needs are met together with a re-enforcing mechanism that guarantees fulfilment.

As a duty, the man and woman must show interest and concern for each other in all spheres of life; their basic needs including food, clothing, shelter and gainful employment must be a concern for both. Their health needs must always be attended to. Discussions and suggestions on how each problem should be tackled are necessary to strengthen one another daily towards the achievement of their set goals.

These are ideals which are, in practice, very difficult to attain particularly when communication between spouses do come to a dead end for one reason or the other. Most often, it is lack of adequate sexual interaction. Sexual interaction is a natural binding mechanism through which couples could refresh their relationship.

Relationships within the family are known to be influenced by the type of family. Some of the family forms in existence include the polygynous family comprising man with more than one wife and their children, a monogamous family of a man his wife and children, single parent families and families from consensual unions. When relationships in families turn sour, family members are able to make-up again sometimes attending social gatherings together or getting one or two friends around and having discussions over a cup of tea in the very sophisticated homes, or even over a bowl of "fufu" or "akple" depending on the occasion and the preference of the visiting friends or relations. Sometimes, a drive out of the house to meet and have a chart with friends or relations helps.

As before, there are a lot that religious bodies provide to help resolve such impasse between couples. Some churches have a number of fellowship groups which meet periodically to have the word of God discussed and as the couple attend these meetings and hold discussions voicing out their experiences, they learn from others how to resolve their problems at home and in the process, others, may also learn something from those encounters.

In the farming communities, the couple often takes time off their busy hours to cook on the farm. There, it is the man that usually, does the cooking. They sit under the shade of a tree and spend time to enjoy their meal together.

Couples usually feel very blessed if their marriage is fruitful. Their concern for the children begins from the moment the woman announces her pregnancy through the ante-natal care to post-natal and to adulthood. Parental care begins right after birth. By instinct, the mother sets out to protect the baby from the fluctuations in temperature by wrapping the baby in clothes and also keep close to the baby for warmth. The baby, be it boy-child or girl-child, continues to receive attention from the parents, through feeding, bathing, clothing, playing and teaching, until the child begins to develop into adulthood and shows both physical and mental maturity as discussed earlier in this book.

It is imperative that the parents meet all the needs of the child. It is a neglect, on the part of the parents, to be unable to do so, for a child's future could be dampened through a neglect she suffers from her parenting. When parents are able to meet their obligations to their children, they derive a lot of joy and self-satisfaction and they feel fulfilled. On the other hand, if parents fail, they feel very frustrated and disappointed. It must be one of the greatest sins for parents to be unable to fulfill the needs of the children they are responsible for bringing into the world. Parents do feel guilty if they are unable to meet the needs of their children. For, when all goes well with meeting our responsibilities as parents we make the children very happy and confident because they have received our love, which even God demands on us for them.

In spite of all these concerns, it has been observed that capitalism and male domination have managed to survive many different forms of marital, child-bearing and child-rearing relationships (Gaskell 1992). The marital patterns that result are an interplay of what the powerful want and how confident the couple are collectively and individually in their way of getting things done. "While structures of domination define some of the conditions that a new generation confronts the solutions people work out for themselves are not predetermined" (Gaskell 1992: 74). To make this meaningful, there is the need to move away from structural theory to a level where individuals can take decisions for themselves determining the balance between patriarchy and capitalism.

Another essential factor that influences family patterns is the 'socialization theory' which is based on 'sex roles' inherent in our traditional norms and religious exposures. A lot of these influences come through the attitudes of teachers, parents, friends and relatives. These people even though they have experienced parenthood differently continue to impress upon the youth the stereotyped textbook and/or traditional attitudes that prevent the youth from achieving better results in their family lives than they experienced. These protectionist attitudes aimed at better results but yield poorer family lives.

Sexuality and the family are crucial issues for women's rights to equal choice and freedom from fear and oppression. Women's sexual well-being, their emotional and physical security are fundamental to their social well being and to their full participation in their country's social and economic development plans, policies and programmes. Women's sexuality seems to be linked most readily only to their biological ability to reproduce. In many cultures, women's own sexual desire is negated and seen as socially-evil and dangerous to men. Thus, most women have accepted this notion and, therefore, hardly express their desire for sex unless it is initiated by a man. This largely affects their self-fulfillment.

The continuing location of women in the family is central to understanding women's subordination in both capitalist and socialist societies (Gaskell 1992). Marriage continues to bind many women into unequal relationships with men; this inequality is not necessarily a result of the relationship between women and men as such but owes its link to social and economic structures approved by state power.

Marrying other than on the basis of free choice and romantic love exist, particularly, the forms of arranged marriages as practised by many Asians in Britain (Jackson 1993: 191) and in most rural settings in Ghana.

There are no logical or empirical grounds for arguing that choosing a spouse on the basis of romantic love offers any greater guarantee of marital happiness than offered by arranged marriage. Studies on Western marriages show that whether a marriage offers promises such as affection and companionship, togetherness and unity does not necessarily depend on whether the marriage was contracted by the couple themselves based on love and romance or whether the marriage contracted was arranged (Jackson 1993).

Husbands and wives often define togetherness differently. The man may just want a home with a wife — a secure physical and emotional base somewhere and someone to come to, while the woman desires a close exchange of intimacy which will make her to be valued as a person and not just a wife (Jackson 1993: 192).

Women now have a greater choice as to whether or not they just want to have children and cater for them by themselves or to marry under patriarchy or opt out of heterosexual relationships altogether. Women could get trapped into a non-capitalist form of production resulting in master and slave type of relationship where the woman, apart from fulfilling her biological reproductive function also contributes a lot to domestic labour.

The 'domestic ideology' suggests that women should put family matters before their career. Women have an inherent responsibility of keeping their home in such a way as to make it comfortable for their male spouse and visitors to their home. They see most of the work in the home their responsibility rather than that of the men. This ideology merely makes the woman feel different but not necessarily unequal to the man. It goes further to obscure power differences and uses gender rather than choice or achievement as the criterion for determining who does what in the home. This notion has been the trend over the years and goes to the extent that women have become successfully socialized into femininity and they have accepted and prefer to do domestic work and see themselves more suited to domestic chores rather than their male counterparts (Gaskell 1992).

It is, therefore, very common to observe the following characters of many wives: Her main job is doing things that he likes; she makes the home her own and makes it a nice and comfortable place for both of them.

Some wives find the home an alternative place to the stresses of a paid job. Others find it a more rewarding place to spend their time. Yet others feel staying home is the only way to make their marriage work. To them, the benefits outweigh the problems such as loneliness, dependence and boredom.

Even when it comes to raising children, the general consensus is that women are better with the children than the men. Women have softer voices for the baby and for kids at all stages of their development. Children like softness. In a few cases, depending on what love they receive in their childhood, men are equally very good at raising children. The masculinity of men has been seen by women as inconvenient for raising children, others see their masculinity as supportive — the man always have to add his voice to let the child obey an instruction from the woman .

In recent times, most educated women have realized that paid work provides status, money and independence and the ability to control their own lives. They find paid jobs less boring, more socially rewarding and challenging.

Biological differences between men and women and the 'domestic ideology' underlie these perceptions.

Other contributing factors to these perceptions as has been mentioned elsewhere in this book include cultural norms that accept gender differences and the type of patriarchy families experienced. Women have experienced their fathers, brothers and boyfriends involvement in domestic work as special favours rather than as a duty.

Chapter 3

THE CAREER OR WORKING WOMAN

Formal Education of the Girl-Child

Historically, women were accepted as home makers and were relegated to house-hold chores such as cooking and cleaning homes, bearing children and caring for them and also providing labour on farms of their husbands for free or on other farms for a fee or got paid in kind in the form of food supplies. In this state, they were unable to contribute economically to help maintain their homes. Over the years, it became evident that, given the same formal education as the boy-child, the girl-child can be gainfully useful to society and to her home. The need for formal education for the girl-child is receiving much attention in all modern societies. For example, on the eve of the United Nations International Women's Year in 1975, the profile of women was stated as: "Women constitute 50 per cent of the world population and one-third of the world's workforce; they work two-third of the world's working hours, earn one-tenth of the world's income and own one-hundredth of the world's property" (Nikoi 1998: 9). If efforts are directed towards the income levels and property ownership of the world's fifty per cent populace —women, the world's development efforts will definitely result in an upturn.

The many blessings that the formal education of the girl-child unfolds for society are becoming inevitable. Formal education is justified eventually in the attainment of loftier values like critical inquiry, love of knowledge or participation in democratic processes and essentially successful family lives; which could be measured for a woman by her success at motherhood.

The formal educational system is an agency through which individual personalities are trained to be motivationally and technically adequate to perform adult roles. It provides an agency for socializing the working class and helps develop new attitudes to working and raising the standard of living in their homes. This socialization is the development in individuals of the commitments and capacities which are essential prerequisites of the performance of their future roles.

Commitments may be to the implementation of the broad values of society or a commitment to the performance of specific type of role within the structure of society. Capacities could also be seen in two perspectives. First, the efficiency of the skill to perform the tasks involved in the individual's roles and secondly, the capacity to live up to other people's expectations of the inter-personal behaviour appropriate to these roles — both in our professions and in our families.

In spite of what the formal educational system provides it is, from the point of view of the society, an agency for 'manpower' allocation that dictates our behaviour, our efforts and our concerns. If society clings to its religious and cultural values and differentiates between what is good and acceptable as against what is bad and demeaning, our behaviour becomes directed towards those acts that are good and acceptable in society. Some of the negative behaviour traits include fornication, adultery, prostitution, stealing or telling lies about an issue or someone, witchcraft and possession of other evil powers.

Thus, formal education in its broad sense has a very wide scope. Apart from facilitating the training of the girl in the various professional areas which hitherto were male-dominated, it also provides the needed exposure to values of family life as enshrined within conventional religious practices and cultural norms.

Most often, formal education is offered in the classroom but needs to be largely supported in the homes. Usually, when family systems are well structured and there exists interaction among the families, children are able to learn towards their adult life through such close interaction with their parents and other family members. Sometimes, however, these interactions are almost non-existent and children, both boys and girls, only learn from or depend on teachings from textbooks and literature available to them from their homes or libraries.

Different Working Mothers

The labour market is a site of complex inter-related inequalities which are linked to and reinforced by factors such as gender and unequal access to education and training (Witz 1993: 272). These factors affect women's choice of jobs, the terms on which women participate in paid employment and also opportunities for women's advancement. In Ghana, women's participation in the job market is also highly influenced by high incidence of early marriages and teenage pregnancies. According to a situation analysis conducted jointly by the Republic of Ghana and the UN Children Fund in 1990, it was recorded that 86 per cent of women operate in the unskilled labour market of wholesale and retail trade and 89 per cent of women were involved in sales, while women constitute 51 per cent of people involved in small-scale cottage industries.

Women are involved both in the private and public spheres of work. "There are clearly links and interconnections between women's work in the 'private' sphere of the household and the 'public' sphere of paid work" (Witz 1993: 273). Women have made up a steadily increasing proportion of the total labour force over the past fifty to sixty years in most industrialized capitalist societies. For example, in 1982, Canada recorded 40.9 per cent, France 38.6 per cent, UK 39.1 per cent and USA 42.8 per cent of the female share of labour force made up of the population aged 15–64 (Witz 1993: 275).

In Ghana, women's participation in the educational disciplines which prepares them for the labour market has undergone varying proportions to that of their men folk. The highest rate of female participation in education has been one female to every four males in the 1980s as against one female to every sixteen men in the 1970s. A UNICEF/Government of Ghana (1990) report shows a generally high literacy rates in both sexes mainly between the ages 15 and 34 years but recorded a rapid fall for women in succeeding age groups and that only one-quarter of all females can read and write while 40 per cent of the male population could read and write. In the 1990s, female participation rates in academia improved favourably in all the disciplines. There was one to five males in the arts-based disciplines and education; two to eleven in the science-based research units; one to seven in the social-science-based and non-science-based research units (Brown *et. al.* 1996a).

In Ghana, women have trained to participate in politics, hold executive positions and be represented in the academia. In politics, there were no women representation during the initial stages of Ghana's First Republic (Brown *et. al.* 1996a). However, during the second phase of the Second Republic, between 2.0 per cent and 7.2 per cent of parliamentarians were women. This increased to 9.5 per cent in 1990's. In the Fourth Republic, 16 out of 200 parliamentarians were women and 3 women were members of the Council of State. There were 3 women Cabinet Ministers out of 19 Ministers. Out of 10 Regional Ministers, there were two women and out of 50 Deputy Ministers, there were five women.

In the year 2000, the last year of President J. J. Rawlings administration, there were women parliamentarians, women Ministers, women Deputy Ministers and women serving on the Council of State. As parliamentarians, they actively participated in parliamentary debates and proceedings and moved motions. Women were members of almost all the Committees of Parliament but in rather scanty numbers. Women's participation in politics in Ghana is, however, yet to reach the critical mass of 33 per cent recommended in the Report of the Secretary-General to the Economic and Social Council in 1995 (Brown *et. al.* 1996a).

In the executive positions in the Civil Service, women's participation has been low. In 1996, there were only 11.1 per cent of women in executive positions within the Civil Service. This was an increase of 4.2 per cent over the 1976/77 figure. In the 1960s only one woman was recorded as Departmental Head in Ghana Radio and Television Department of the Ministry of Information (Brown *et. al.* 1996a).

In 'High Level Manpower' (i.e. people trained up to at least University degree or its equivalent) survey in the 1970s conducted by CSIR discovered that there was a very low representation of women. The areas of studies covered in the survey included economics, accountancy, computer science, the social sciences, education and documentation, engineering, biological and physical sciences, mathematics, agriculture, architecture as well as town, country and physical planning. The results of this study revealed that only 0.5 per cent of the engineers were women, 20 per cent of the personnel in the biological sciences were women. Women in documentation were 11.38 per cent. Documentation covered librarianship, archives and archaeology. There were 9.3 per cent and 7.1 per cent of women in the social sciences and agriculture respectively (Brown *et. al.* 1996a).

Again in the academia, women were more highly represented in the lecturer's rank than in all other ranks. On the whole, women's participation has been low. For example, in the three premier universities (University of Ghana, University of Cape Coast and Kwame Nkrumah University of Science and Technology) only 12.1 per cent were women lecturers in the 1990s. Within the professorial rank, only 5.1 per cent were women (Brown *et al.* 1996a).

In the 1960s, the then existing three universities, University of Ghana (Legon), University of Science and Technology (UST) and University College of Cape Coast (UCC) recorded 409 academic staff out of which 11.7 per cent were women.

On the continent of Africa, an ECA-sponsored publication: *Status and Role of women in East Africa* in 1964, revealed that "women often carried a major portion of economic burden . . . at the same time, they occupied an honoured position and exerted much power and influence in society" (Snyder and Tadesse 1995: 31.)

By mid to late 1960s other research findings verified women's

TABLE 1

Summary Distribution of Academic Staff by Rank and Gender (1960s)

	Males	Females	Grand Total	% F	Ratio F:M
Professor	39	1	40	2.5	1:39
Associate Professor	28	4	32	12.5	1:7
Senior Lecturer	69	3	72	4.17	1:23
Lecturer	244	34	278	12.2	1:7
Assistant Lecturer	29	12	41	29.3	2:5
Total	409	54	463	11.7	9:68

Source: Extracted from Table 3.5 in Brown et. al. 1996a.

centrality not only to social but also to economic progress in the different African countries. For example:

1. In Lesotho, 90 per cent of road building under the food-for-work programme was done by women.

2. In Gabon, women worked 200 days a year in the fields while men spend few, if any, days there.

3. In Tanzania, men worked 1,800 hours as compared with women's 2,600 hours annually in agriculture.

4. In Uganda, the Faculty of Agriculture at Makerere University was established in the late 1930s but it was only in 1967 that the first two women were enrolled.

5. Women represented 60 per cent of the sellers in urban markets in Dakar in 1959, 66 per cent in Brazzaville Bacongo in 1962, 83 per cent in Lagos in 1960; 85 per cent in Accra, in 1959 (Snyder and Tadesse 1995).

These are the underlying facts that continue to help transform the leftover colonial images of women in Africa into realistic ones.

The birth of the United Nations Economic Commission for Africa (ECA) in the late 1950s brought with it a unique opportunity for women to strengthen their positions. The ECA tenet conceived the 'women and development' approach which was based on the fact that women's economic and family contributions as well as women's needs were linked up with the priority needs and aspirations of the Africa region.

The job positions held by women determine their income levels. Over the years, the few formal sector jobs remained the domain of men. Women often find seasonal labour in agriculture while others enter the informal sector — micro enterprise and trade where their incomes do not meet their requirements. Low educational levels direct women into the informal sector.

The myth of the male breadwinner suppresses the truth about who exactly is responsible for the family, for it is women's lives that are shaped by family obligations. Women are known to spend more of their earnings on family needs than men do and in most African families one-third of all households, on average, have the woman as the sole breadwinner. Ghana recorded 32.2 per cent of households headed by women in 1988; Zimbabwe 32.6 per cent in 1989 whilst Botswana recorded 45.9 per cent in 1988 (Snyder and Tadesse 1995: 203).

Thus, economic empowerment means not just increasing labour productivity or earning money but also controlling the products and income from the labour. This underlies the status of women and the well-being of their families. Women enjoy a rise in their status from their husbands when they earn incomes and use them for the benefit of the family. Unfortunately, this is also a point of disagreement for some 'brothers' who judge their sister's contribution to her home as her enslavement and not a joy and a privilege to do so.

Educational opportunity and economic empowerment have not come about automatically. They have been effected through professional and political action by both men and women in civil society, through the educational system and by institutions described as the instruments of change.

Women Specialized Groups

Women's savings, production, marketing and mutual aid groups exist and offered solidarity assistance to women. Since the 1970s, there has been a surge in specialized groups formed by lawyers, businesswomen, bankers, home economists and other professionals. Some of these groups and organs in Ghana are discussed presently.

Federacion Internacional de Abogada (FIDA)
FIDA Ghana is the Ghana chapter of the International Federation of Women Lawyers. FIDA Ghana has the main objective of enhancing and promoting the welfare of women and children. This is done through organizing seminars, workshops and public lectures during which women are educated on their legal, social, political and economic rights. FIDA is financially assisted by donor agencies such as Friedrich Ebert Foundation (FES) (Duncan 1997).

The National Council on Women and Development (NCWD)
The National Council on Women and Development (NCWD) came into being by an NRC Decree (NRCD 322) in response to the UN Resolution 961. This resolution drew the attention of member nations to the need to set up national commissions to oversee the improvement in the status and roles of women in the world community. Each country was to develop action plans that would lead to the improvement of the position of women in their respective countries (Brown et. al. 1996b: 13).

NCWD is guided in its activities by the 1975 Mexico Declaration which set out to ensure the full participation of women in national development — in education, healthcare and policy-making. Recently, its activities have been influenced by the Beijing Conference of 1995. NCWD addresses issues such as customary beliefs, prejudices and practices on advancement of women in educational and economic areas. It also serves as an official body for the co-operating, co-ordinating and liaising with national and international organizations on matters relating to the status of women.

The NCWD has assisted several women's groups in collaboration with governmental, non-governmental and international agencies. Their income generation programme has been particularly effective in strengthening the work of some rural women's groups. For example, the Technologies for Rural Women's Project has succeeded in lessening the expenditure of labour on and improving the quality of soap-making, oil extraction, fish smoking and gari processing.

The Thirty-First December Womens' Movement
The 31st DWM was established during the PNDC era and has been concentrating a lot of its efforts in obtaining foreign sponsorship for women in the agro-processing business. The Movement has been interested in political activities. Its leadership has been active in political conscientization of the members at the local level and has succeeded in involving many women District assembly members as its members.

The Movement has become a potent vehicle for womens' development in political participation at the grass root level (Brown et. al. 1996b: 13). Apart from organizing and supporting rural women's groups in their productive activities, the Movement also helps in conscientizing women about their status and place in society. It has succeeded in setting up day-care centres and creches in both urban and rural areas to cater for the needs of children and reduce women's work and concerns.

Ghana Federation of Business and Professional Women (GFBPW)
The Ghana Federation of Business and Professional Women (GFBPW) is an affiliate of the International Federation of Business and Professional Women (IFBPW). It was formed in 1976 and registered in 1981 to respond to the needs of women who are often marginalized.

The aims of the Federation are:

1. To stimulate in women a positive attitude towards themselves and the society at large.

2. To promote equal opportunities and status for women in economic, social and political life in the country thus removing all forms of discrimination against and among women.

3. To encourage women and girls to acquire education to the highest possible level and to create and enhance their entrepreneurial ability.

4. To help women attain a high standard of service in their businesses and professions.

5. To encourage good record keeping so as to enable women to make use of banking facilities for business growth.

The Federation works toward these goals throughout the country by organizing workshops and seminars on various issues relating to women in business and the professions.

Activities of the Federation are funded by donor agencies and at present there are 15 clubs all over the country with the headquarters in Accra. Each Club consists of members and five Executive Officers while the National Board is made of the National President and six Executive Officers. Membership is open to all literate women who are actively engaged in business or a profession and are willing to volunteer time, finance and expertise to the aims of the Federation.

Florence Dolphyne emphasizing the need to establish womens' influence within the government and the political party structures said: "The creation of women's bureaux and councils in various African countries has meant a focus on women's issues at the national level to a degree not known in any of these countries before 1975" (Snyder and Tadesse 1995: 188).

Each profession makes a special demand on the personality of the woman both technically and socially. The success of the woman is the right interplay of her technical and social roles.

Greater Participation of Women

Advantages and Benefits
The need to increase the level of women's participation has been recognized by many. Women's interest and perceptions are more likely to bear on decisions at high managerial or professional levels than their male counterparts. Ignoring women or neglecting them is an oppression that does not only deprive them as individuals but deprives society as a whole of their distinct skill and differing experiences in life. The Secretary General of Economic and Social Council (1995) issued a report that set the reasonable level of women's participation called the "critical mass" at 30–35 per cent (Brown *et. al.* 1996a). It is reported that so far it is the Nordic countries which have attained such a level. The impact on their society is very commendable. Women have control over their own bodies. Sexual violence is minimized and their men give them a lot of assistance in child care (Brown *et. al.* 1996a).

It has been observed in a study conducted by Development and Women's Study(DAWS) in 1995 that women exhibit excellent professional qualities when they are trained in professions earlier on reserved for men. It was noticed that children both sons and daughters of highly-educated and financially secure women are able to receive higher education and aspire to high professional levels (Brown *et. al.* 1996a).

As a long term effect, women's participation in public life also sets the stage for a role model and is a pre-requisite for motivating the younger females both in training or in the prime of their career. A greater participation of women in all levels of governance is also a good measure of the level of democracy in the political life of a country.

Some problems of greater participation of women

The relevance of the full participatory role of a woman in the home cannot be over emphasized. Her role in the home and in the society at large is like that of a bird flying with all its wings and without her role, the home or the society operates like that bird which flies on only one wing. That home or society in that plight necessarily will need other supportive measures to keep it on course.

Gender discrimination often stems from traditional and conservative cultural practices and attitudes and religious concepts and interpretations. These concepts often invariably perceived the women as subordinates to men. Unfortunately, these notions have been imbibed in the moral fabric of the women themselves and they themselves so accept them in their various cultural and religious setups so much so that they no longer see them as problems but as the rights of their male counterparts. Instead of tradition amending discriminatory practices, tradition is often involved in interfering with women's participatory roles in society. Over the years, observations show that religious interpretations play a significant role in determining cultural attitudes that promote or inhibit the participatory role of women.

The girls are usually raised to identify with the family and the private sphere while boys are brought up to act in the public sphere. Education which sets out to narrow this cultural and traditional gap also has its shortcomings. School activities are gender stereotyped and educational materials or programmes are gender characterized. The resultant educated girl who evolves from these programmes is seen, if not too polite, refined, shy and too submissive to men then she is too arrogant, sophisticated and unmarriageable.

In Ghana, no laws ban women from participation in education, public service, and in politics. However, there are numerous obstacles that have been identified to inhibit women's full participation in these spheres of life. Ghartey (1992) identified these inhibitory factors which he called 'prop factors'. These factors are identified as follows:

1. Poor or complete lack of education and training for effective performance in the modern sectors of the political economy;
2. The impact of existing cultural thought models — in Akan areas; birth of boys is more welcome than the birth of girls;
3. The social structure which accepts male dominance;
4. Female apathy or inhibition;
5. Male chauvinism, superiority complex and lack of sympathy;

6. Religious and cultural influences; and
7. The stress from economic conditions.

Beyond these, even among the élite, it is noticed that the woman is deprived of important rights and responsibilities in the community and she may not be aware of her rights under the law. The woman often faces legal discrimination and restrictions that inhibit her participation in many spheres of life. Constitutional and legislative guarantees of women's rights are not always implemented and religious laws, customary or personal status laws that discriminate against women may be allowed to over-ride such constitutional declarations and legislation. For example, marital laws in Ghana have concessions for men to practise polygamy, while women are not permitted to practise polyandry.

In situations where there is a recognition of women's rights, there is still the need to increase the awareness of such rights. Where there is no such recognition, the need to raise awareness for the purpose of agitating for such rights becomes necessary.

Legal guarantees and knowledge of one's rights are not sufficient unless these rights are capable of being enforced. People also need the means to be able to claim their rights and the woman must have equal access to the justice system. The woman seems to have the conditional access to the "four freedoms" which the universal declarations of human rights and the subsequent human right covenants aspire to define as freedom from fear, freedom from want, freedom of speech and freedom of belief.

In recent years, violence against women, in its many forms, has come to be recognized as a major obstacle to women's participation. Violence in any form or the threat of it, both in its blatant or subtle form prevents women from being active and causes them to pull back from participation.

A United Nations Development Fund for Women (UNIFEM) paper reported that violence against women is often a direct obstacle to women's participation in development programmes. In my opinion, violence against women can be defined as acts, attitudes and perceptions which militate against and inhibit the development of the full potential of the woman. Maynard (1993) gives three definitions of violence:

1. **Legal definition:** This requires the intervention or prosecution by authorities such as the police, social services and courts of law. Under this, certain acts of violence which otherwise could

be considered violent may tend to be omitted. For example, in Britain until 1990, the law protected men raping their wives and covered them because wives had consented to sexual intercourse with the man on marriage. In many states in the US and parts of Australia and most of Scandinavia, sexual intercourse without a wife's consent was considered a rape; unlawful sexual intercourse does not include forcible penetration by other objects and other forms of sex such as anal intercourse.

Legal definitions of child sexual abuse and pornography, incest, vary in different countries. Some countries call father-daughter rapes as incest, others adopt incest in a wider sense to include all abuse committed with the family or by any relative, however distant (Maynard 1993: 102).

Even though the law is expected to be gender-neutral, its power lies in the ability to decide what does and does not comprise a violent act. Unfortunately, it has been observed by feminist opinion that this power often rather protects the interest of men and not that of women. The law often discounts the views of women giving legitimacy to their male assailants and upholds the right of men to abuse women.

2. **Professional/expert definition**: In this definition, the views of professionals and experts such as doctors and child psychologists are paramount. These experts can establish after a thorough professional examination that there has been a violence or not. This can be established regardless of what the law accepts as violence or what the victim women or young females accept as violence. This definition can be criticized for not including the idea that force or the threat of force may be used.

The notion of 'informed consent' is also problematic for feminists since it assumes that the ability to say 'yes' or 'no' in abusive situations is a relatively straightforward affair, when, in fact, it is frequently complicated by relationships of power and emotional blackmail, developmentally immature and sexual actions. There is a dispute as to what constitutes sexual action with regard to younger females and the implication of consent and complicity with regard to older females.

3. **Women's definition**: The 'radical feminist' perspective argues that in order to be able to capture the extent of the impact of violence upon women it is important not to pre-determine the meaning of the term. It is, therefore, necessary to know about women's experiences of violence and the boundaries which they draw around them. By this Liz Kelly (Maynard 1993) was able to establish that what women experience as children or adults is neither covered under the legal or the professional definition. Some of these experiences include threats, sexual harassment, pressure to have sex and coercive sex.

These challenge the notion that all sexual intercourse which are not defined as rape are, therefore, consensual. Other forms of abuse or attack can influence women's lives. For example, abusive behaviour and language from either boys or girls in a school setup or a workplace with sexual connotation can alienate some girls from education and learning.

According to Diane Hudson, even professionals have been able to use threats of hospitalization, electro-convulsive therapy and psychosurgery to control women's behaviour and confine it to channels acceptable to men (Maynard 1993: 106).

Sexual violence is defined to include: "any physical, visual or sexual act that is experienced by the woman or girl, at the same time or later, as a threat, invasion or assault, that has the effect of hurting her or degrading her and/or takes away her ability to control intimate contact" (Maynard 1993: 106).

Sexual harassment involves a variety of behaviour, some involving physical contact, some of a verbal or psychological kind ranging from suggestive remarks which could come even from fellow women, looks or joking, unwanted touching or patting to direct sexual propositioning — it is not mutual; it is not welcome; it offends and it threatens. These acts could direct a girl or woman to changing her attitude to family life, or changing her route to school or changing her mind about her workplace.

We do not intend to go into the explanations for male violence against women. Their reasons could be liberal/psychological, social, structural or feminist in nature.

Most often, violence is domestic and it is experienced as either sexual harassment or sexual starvation and lack of affection, lack of finance, physical assaults and the like, which militates and inhibits the development of the full potential in women as wives and mothers.

Other obstacles that hamper the development of the full potential of women include:

1. Household status;
2. Employment and remuneration;
3. Work-related rights (maternity leave, job security, provision for child-care);
4. Double burden of work;
5. Education and literacy;
6. Peculiar feminine ill-health;
7. Ability to control fertility;
8. Access to financial resources;
9. Legal rights;
10. Traditional and cultural attitudes;
11. Religious concepts; attitudes and practices;
12. The mass media and other false and offensive publications on women;
13. Socialization and self-confidence;
14. Wife-beating, rape, child sexual abuse and sexual harassment;
15. Rights to divorce and legal separation on grounds of husbands' violence;
16. Male violence and control over women's sexuality and reproduction;
17. Female circumcision; and
18. In India, dowry deaths — wives are killed by husbands and in-laws for not providing sufficient money or goods on marriage (Maynard 1993: 100).

Observations in Africa indicate that a woman's labour is a controlled labour force. When a woman fails to comply with social activities associated with her work, such as, house chores, mothering, provision of sexual and emotional services, she faces physical, financial and social difficulties. A higher value is put on her traditional role as a female than on all other achievements in education and career. Thus, most women are pulled away from participation in public life in order to fulfil the demands on their marriage and motherhood while those who remain in public life have had to make compromises to cope with the varied roles they have to play or sacrifice their marriage.

It is noticeable, even in developed societies like the US, that the woman is excluded from acquiring, from among her work colleagues, informal power which she needs to develop as a network of other relationships to enhance her work and to facilitate her attainment of higher managerial positions.

In Ghana, more women are found in the informal than in the formal sector which offers higher status and a rise to higher offices. Higher office positions facilitate participation in decision-making (Brown et. al. 1996a).

The intervention by the NCWD for the inclusion of women on all boards of institutions and corporations is a right step to break the myth. Observations show that women are increasingly participating in technical, professional and administrative positions. Thus, we have a good representation of women as doctors, lawyers, accountants, engineers, agriculturists, veterinarians, etc. A number of women are still in the female fields such as nursing, teaching, secretarial jobs, sewing, hair-dressing, catering and house-keeping. However, it is noted that their number at the managerial levels is still inadequate to enable them to have the needed impact on decision-making and influence the many issues that affect women. Dolphyne asserted that it is only women who can effectively resolve their own problems (Dolphyne 1991).

The norms, beliefs, customs and organizational practices reflect male culture with the opinion that the female is different. Chieftaincy institutions are male dominated (Brown et. al. 1996b: 16). The establishment of the institution of queenmothers is a step to help women get involved in decisions on marriages, funerals, establishment of schools, clinics, market places and community centres. I hope that the recent refusal of most chiefs to allow the queenmothers to participate in the deliberation of the house of chiefs would be reversed since the queenmothers have a lot to offer especially with regard to issues concerning women.

Other male views on women undermine their capabilities, attributes, roles and aspirations. These notions demand that the woman work harder than her male counterparts to attain the same managerial position. Two types of the career woman evolve: a hard-working one who is branded infeminine and the in-between-type who is divided between her career and her personal life, also branded as non-committed. During recruitments, few women are taken and those within an organization move at a slower pace than their male counterparts. They are unable to accept postings which will promote their attainment of higher positions for fear of losing their spouses or male sexual partners.

Most of those hindrances evolve from inherent social practices in the home which all the time define gender roles. We will need to minimize the effects of these notions right from the home, exposing both the male and female child to any chore in the home provided his/her physical strength could support such a chore.

Towards the Improvement of Problems of Women

An attempt to ameliorate the plight of women and to enhance their meaningful participation in development cannot ignore offering the necessary tools. These tools include access to the means of production namely, land, education, credit, technology, farm inputs, storage, labour markets, infrastructure development and extension services. The discussion here considers only land, education and credit.

Organizations such as the 31st December Women's Movement, The National Council for Women and Development (NCWD), FIDA and Women's World Banking, have various logistics in place to provide the needed infrastructure and to facilitate the access to most of the means of production for women.

Access to Land

Historically, women did not play any traditional role in land acquisition. Since land was obtained through conquest or appropriation under stool land leadership or lineage head, women had no role to play since they were usually not heads in stool land administration, not even in matrilineal systems where the woman is presumed to be the head of the family (Duncan 1997).

Stools, generally, possess the highest title to land under the Allodial Title and stool subjects and lineage members of either sex have inherent rights to these lands but in practice women have only usufractory holds on these lands and men play a more prominent role in such land ownerships (Duncan 1997).

The contributing factors include early marriage and its attendant marital and domestic obligations, the gender patterns in division of labour which clearly enables men to be given priority and prominence in land acquisition while the woman become food and firewood collector only, financial ability for land development which women did not have; the emergence of permanent crops, such as cocoa, production of which was by men; the replacement of owners through the acquisition of stool and lineage lands by rich strangers and multinational corporations for large sums of money.

Studies under the Women in Agriculture (WIA) survey discovered that women are able to acquire land commonly through pleading as in the northern Ghana, share cropping as in Brong Ahafo; inheritance as in Ashanti Region; licence and user right of husband's land or free use as in Brong Ahafo. Women hardly could acquire land through purchase — they could not afford it or land was not saleable to women (Duncan 1997: 75).

Although, the tide is changing and a few women can afford to own land, and now own land and immoveable property the percentage is still very low.

Access to Education
Formal education empowers women. By increasing women's ability to earn an independent income, education increases women's status in the community and leads to greater input into family and community decision-making.

More importantly, formal education provides women with a basic knowledge of their rights as individuals and as citizens of their nation and the world. Possession of knowledge, income and decision-making power can place women on a more equal footing with their male counterparts.

Formal education also provides knowledge and skills to contribute to and benefit from development efforts especially in areas of health, nutrition, water and sanitation, the environment and family forms. Efforts in these areas are more likely to be successful if women understand the new concepts and their potential benefits, possess the skills needed to implement new ideas and are willing to test these concepts with their families and communities.

Girls' formal education is a necessary condition to ensure that development efforts will be sustained because girls grow into adulthood as women. The status of women rises hand in hand with economic and social development. UNICEF reported that 'girls' formal education correlates positively with several important national and international goals, including universal primary education, economic productivity, social development, intergenerational education, social equity and sustainability of development efforts.

The educational policy in Ghana has no gender biases openly and, therefore, all students irrespective of their sexes, could participate in all subjects and can enter any school in the locality. Practices in the various schools, however, gender-determine student's participation in certain professions.

With regard to enrollment into schools, societal attitudes and norms prevent girls from entering in greater numbers like their male counterparts. For example a field survey conducted in 1996 reported female enrollment in government-assisted schools in the Cape Coast area as follows: In Agriculture, out of 403 students 20 per cent were females; in Accounting, out of 1554 students, 28.3 per cent were females; in Secretarial courses, 264 were enrolled and 97 per cent were females; in General Art, 2306 were enrolled and 41.2 per cent were females; in General Science, 2931 were enrolled and only 27.9 per cent were females; in Technical Engineering, 220 were enrolled and only one female was among them representing 0.5 per cent; in Electrical Engineering, 86 were enrolled and there was no female among them. However, with the Vocational Studies such as Home Economics out of the 530 enrolled 98.3 per cent were females and in Visual Art 504 were enrolled and 28.8 per cent were females (Brown et. al. 1996a: 47).

Superficially, both males and females have the same experience in school in their chosen courses. However, in a way their interaction with their teachers at school differs; the male student receives more encouragement from the teachers most of whom are males. The male students have greater chances of holding longer discussions with their teachers, receiving tutorship from them and also receiving specific instructions as to how to get things done than their female counterparts (Brown, Anokye and Britwum 1996). This gives the male a positive booster to good performance academically. A female who attempts to learn more from a male tutor may be disadvantaged and end up becoming his lover; this has a negative influence on her academic performance. The reverse is not the case for boys. Some girls even have to end their education through this kind of relationship. The impact of female teachers in influencing the greater participation of girls at school is very highly recommended.

Access to Credit

The availability of credit is a prerequisite to the scope of performance of any entrepreneur. Thus, the woman as an entrepreneur at home, on her farm, in her trade or business or in her professional practice needs credit to perform economically. Credit will enable her to acquire greater income-yielding plots, pay for labour, purchase the necessary inputs and help improve the nutrition and health of her children at home.

Credit facilities are available formally and informally. The formal credit institutions which provide credit to women include all the financial institutions in Ghana, namely: Agricultural Development Bank, Ghana

Commercial Bank, Standard Chartered Bank, National Investment Bank; Rural Banks, Barclays Bank, Metropolitan and Allied Bank, the Trust Bank, Prudential Bank, among others. They have no open biases towards lending to women but, in practice, the bureaucratic nature of their lending policies only facilitate the participation of men. More men are educated than women and can cope with the bureaucracies. Also, the inability of women to possess properties that can meet the security requirements of the banks is another negative factor.

Today, there are specific institutions such as Women's World Banking, the NCWD and 31st December Women's Movement, National Board for Small-Scale Industries (NBSSI) and the Trades Union Congress (TUC) who arrange for credit needs of the women. The procedures at these institutions allow women a free access to credit, minimized bureaucracy and, therefore, reach women even at the grass root level.

Many women derive their capital from informal sources such as from their husbands, boyfriends, relatives, friends, money-lenders, traders or 'susu' groupings. This informal market avoids bureaucracy; funds are made readily available but are often characterized by very high interest rates which eventually renders the woman beneficiary a perpetual debtor and accounts for the heavy indebtedness of most women traders and farmers.

Chapter 4

RIGHTS CONCERNING MARRIAGE, DIVORCE AND PROPERTY OWNERSHIP FOR WOMEN IN GHANA

Forms of Marriage

Marriage is defined by Kuenyehia (1988) as the means of forming a family unit. It is a formalized or legal union of a man and a woman. She asserts that this union in wedlock bestows upon them a status of husband and wife with its corresponding rights and obligations.

In most African societies, marriage goes beyond the union of just the man and woman and unites the two families of the man and the woman. "It is primarily a union between two families, rather than two individuals" (Dolphyne 1991: 2). Marriages can be said to be institutional arrangements for ensuring the continuation of the family, lineage, clan or race.

Historically, in Ghana, only one form of legally-recognized marriage existed before 1884 and this was marriage under customary law. Customary law marriage unites a man's family and a woman's family and forms a contract between the man and the woman (Offei 1998).

The Ordinance No. 14 of 1884, the Marriage Ordinance amended as Cap. 127 and the Ordinance No. 21 of 1907, the Marriage of Mohammedan Ordinance amended as Cap. 129 brought into being two other statutory forms of marriage. At present, there are, therefore, three forms of marriage recognized by law in Ghana, namely:

1. Marriage under Customary law.
2. Marriage under the Marriage Ordinance.
3. Marriage under Marriage of Mohammedan Ordinance.

However, it is worth noting that in any of these forms of marriage the consent of the families of both parties is very essential for a valid marriage. Marriage in the Ghanaian concept must establish a permanent relationship not only between the two parties but also between family members of both parties. In practice, marriage under Customary Law can be contracted on its own but the other ordinance laws are usually preceded by customary rites of the locality. In contrast, presumption of marriage occurs when a man and a woman live for a considerable length of time, have children and maintain them, move together and hold themselves out as married couple (Offei 1998). This type of marriage lacks the necessary legal

Rights Concerning Marriage, Divorce and Property Ownership

support at the death of a spouse or at the time of divorce or separation. However, there are some provisions made with regard to property, claim of children and maintenance if marriages are contracted legally under either Customary Law or under the Marriage Ordinance (Cap 127) or under Mohammedan Ordinance (Cap 129).

We do not intend to go into the details of the various customary rites but will outline the procedure for contracting marriage under the Marriage Ordinance, and the provisions under the Marriage of Mohammedan Ordinance. We will then discuss the rights and responsibilities and rights on property ownership in marriage and upon divorce. We will also discuss the Intestate Succession Law (PNDC Law 111), which is applicable in case of death of a spouse without a will.

Marriage under the Ordinance

Under the Marriage Ordinance (Cap 127) any one of the two parties, the man or woman, to marry is allowed to sign the Registrar's certificate. This certificate gives notice about the intended marriage and it is usually done three months before the date of the marriage ceremony. Both illiterates and literates can sign the certificate. In the case of the former, a fingerprint is acceptable before a literate person who shall attest the same while the literate just appends his/her signature. The registrar supplies the forms of notice. Upon receipt of the notice, the registrar makes entries into the marriage notice book and also publishes such notice on the outer door of his office or on notice board outside his office and keeps the notices there for the three-month period.

A certificate is issued, after twenty-one days of the notice, that is before the expiry of the three months provided the following conditions are fulfilled;

1. That at least one of the parties has been resident within the district in which the marriage is intended at least fifteen days preceding the granting of the certificate.

2. That each of the parties attain the age twenty-one (excludes widower and widow) and if any is under age the consent is made in writing and annexed to an affidavit.

3. That there is not any impediment of kindred or affinity or any other lawful hindrance to the marriage.

4. That none of the parties intending the marriage is married by native law or custom to any person other than the person with whom the marriage is proposed to be contracted.

If the marriage ceremony does not come on within three months of filing the notice, the notice is considered null and void and a fresh notice has to be issued.

For a marriage officer's certificate, each party of the marriage shall, four days before the publication of the banns of marriage, deliver a notice in writing to the marriage officer in the district of his/her residence at least fifteen days before the notice. Also provided that the two have been members of the same religious denomination for the past fifteen days, a single notice can be given and banns of marriage can be published in their place of worship and in the town or village of their residence. One marriage officer's certificate is enough for the solemnization of the marriage.

The marriage officer can publish the banns of marriage or shall cause such banns to be published by some body duly authorized for the purpose in writing by the marriage officer or by endorsing the necessary form.

Banns could be separately published if separate notices are made. These publications are usually in English or in the vernacular of request during Sunday morning worship for three consecutive Sundays. A person desiring to forbid a marriage by banns may enter into a caveat against the issue of a registrar's or marriage officer's certificate. Any relative who has any good reason against such a proposal of marriage should at this time voice it out kindly to the party he/she is protecting or enter into a caveat. Beyond this, all a relation or friend could do is to be supportive and assist the marriage to work out.

A registrar or marriage officer cannot issue his certificate until such caveat is removed. Caveats are usually referred to the Judge of the nearest divisional court. The caveat could be removed at the discretion of the Judge; otherwise the parties are summoned to establish the just cause. Compensations and costs may be awarded to the party injured if the caveat was entered on insufficient ground. The Judges decision on this is final.

In lieu of a caveat, the registrar or marriage officer proceeds to issue the marriage certificate.

The Governor issues his special license upon proof made to him by affidavit that there is no lawful impediment to the proposed marriage and

Rights Concerning Marriage, Divorce and Property Ownership

that the necessary consents has been obtained. This license authorizes the celebration of the marriage.

The celebration could be in a place other than a licensed place of worship or a registrar's office if the Governor so authorizes. Marriage celebrations are permitted between the hour of 8 am and 6 pm in the presence of two or more witnesses besides the officiating minister.

The minister is not expected to conduct a marriage ceremony if any impediments are brought to his notice. After the celebration, the following entries are made in the marriage certificate:

1. The number of the certificate.
2. The date of marriage.
3. The names of the parties.
4. Whether full age or minor.
5. Condition, whether bachelor or widower, spinster or widow.
6. Occupation, rank or profession.
7. Residence at time of marriage
8. Father's/ Mother's name, if known, their occupation, if known.

The names of the witnesses are also entered on the counterfoil. The officiating minister then duly signs the certificates in duplicate. The certificates are also signed by the parties and by two or more witnesses. One certificate is given to the parties and within seven days, the other is transmitted to the registrar of marriages for the particular district for filing.

Marriage can be contracted before a registrar in the presence of two witnesses in his office with open doors between 10.00 am and 4.00 pm on any weekday not being a public holiday.

Marriage contracted under the Marriage Ordinance is strictly monogamous whilst marriage under the Customary Law alone is potentially polygynous.

Marriage under Mohammedans Ordinance (Cap 129)

The Mohammedans Ordinance (Cap 129) provides for the registration of Mohammedan marriages celebrated in Ghana after the commencement of the Ordinance (Sections 5 and 6), and also for the registration of Mohammedan divorces effected in Ghana after the enforcement of the Ordinance.

It also regulates the succession to Mohammedans whose marriages were registered under the Ordinance Section 10. Thus, a Mohammedan marriage, which is not contracted under the provisions of this law, is not recognizable and succession formalities cannot be enforced unless the marriage is proven to be valid under the Customary Law. This Ordinance is hardly enforced; its existence is almost unknown.

Rights in Marriage

Even though Marriage Ordinance has been in existence since 1884, most marriages, particularly in rural settings, are contracted under Customary Law.

Under Customary law, polygyny is allowed. Polygyny served in the past, as a source of agricultural labour. The Customary Law allows the man to have more than one wife but has no such provision for the woman. Thus, children from different mothers can be claimed by the father but children of the wife for the man are only those born to him in the marriage and the man has no legal claim on children the wife had before marrying him.

Observations held, generally, indicate that the relationship that exists between husband and wife emphasized that the woman held an inferior position in comparison to that of the man (Duncan 1997: 107). The woman was under a strict obligation to assist the man in all his endeavours and there was no corresponding obligation on the man to reciprocate this responsibility.

Under the Customary Law, because marriage could be contracted any time after puberty, say at 15 years, the woman is usually very dependent on the man. Early marriage also deprives the young wife, the chances of being able to acquire property of her own, and also prevent her from having an equal access to stool or lineage land (Duncan 1997: 108).

Another feature of the Customary Law is that, the concept of separateness or individualism occurs. There is separateness of both identity and property acquisition. Each party owns what he/she acquires through his/her efforts before and during the marriage. Thus, a woman does not become a member of her husband's lineage farms even though she must have been involved in contributing to improvement on such farms.

Other rights in marriage include:

1. the marriage can only be set aside by a decree of nullity pronounced by a court of competent jurisdiction;

2. the marriage cannot be discharged by agreement, frustration or breach. Apart from death, it can be terminated only by a decree of dissolution by a competent court;

3. the spouses' mutual rights and duties are fixed by law and not by agreement. Variations may be allowed by consent in cases such as release from cohabitation;

4. the power for a wife to apply to court for maintenance in the event of divorce cannot be contracted and the spouses cannot agree to empower the husband to sue his wife in tort (i.e. trespass, nuisance, enticement and slander).

Customary Law requires the consent of the two families concerned to any marital relationship between a man and a woman. Thus, the man who wants to marry applies to the girl's family through his own family. His family, therefore, consents when they present the gifts which vary from tribe to tribe and also according to the means of the man. The girl's family also consents when they receive the gifts on behalf of the girl. The absence of consent from families creates problems when a spouse dies intestate or when there is a divorce; the union could be taken as that of presumption and the wife considered a concubine (Offei 1998).

Other rights allow the husband to claim damages in the event of his wife's infidelity from the co-respondent. Further, the husband has the right to profit by the fruits of her labour and later that of the children in the same way as the husband is liable for his wife's debts and torts and for the maintenance of the wife as well as the children. The wife, however, is not liable for the torts of the husband.

A woman, as stated earlier, does not become a member of her husband's lineage farms even though she must have been involved in contributing to the improvement on such farms.

In the Akim areas, however, 50 per cent of the woman's acquired property during marriage belongs to the man (Duncan 1997). According to Offei (1998), a man has no control over his wife's money and any extra money she can extract from him for herself can never be reclaimed. It is the duty of the man to set the wife up in a trade and the wife has a right to enter into contracts with third parties to promote her trade or business.

Until a few decades ago, the man was regarded as the breadwinner and must maintain his wife and children. In a few cases, women are sole breadwinners or joint breadwinners with their husbands. The Law presumes that any property acquired during the marriage belonged to the man and ignores the interest of the woman who assists the husband in acquiring the property. Ollenu J. said:

> Again by customary law it is a domestic responsibility of a man's wife and children to assist him in carrying out the duties of his station in life, for example, farming or business. The proceeds of this effort of a man and his wife and/or children and any property which the man acquires with such proceeds are by customary law the individual property of the man. It is not the joint property of the man and the wife and/or the children. The right of the wife and the children is a right to maintenance and support from the husband and father (quoted from Offei 1998: 340).

In the same way, even after death, the widow remains the property of the deceased husband's family and has the right to maintenance and support for her and her children until she opts to marry outside the family or continues in marriage with an appointed member of the deceased husband's family.

The right to property in marriage does not seem to favour the woman even if she and her children helped in acquiring the property. The only claim open to a widow of a marriage in Customary Law is the claim for maintenance and support.

As a general rule in the Ghanaian society, the woman is responsible for all household chores and it is a taboo or uncommon to involve husbands in domestic work.

Customary marriage also has peculiar rules with regards to child claim. In patrilineal areas such as the Volta and Northern Regions, children traditionally belong to the man's family whereas in matrilineal areas such as Ashanti and Brong Ahafo areas, the children belong to the family of the woman (Duncan 1997: 112).

It seems, therefore, that since customary rites are prerequisites to the marriages under the Marriage Ordinance, most rights in marriage are traceable to what pertains in the traditional society. The Customary Law makes no commitment or prohibition on the creation of joint property ownerships.

At the courts, a woman was able to recover possession of a property she used her money to purchase in the name of her husband (Court of Appeal 1906). The husband was considered as holding the property as a trustee for the wife even though the conveyance was made to him alone. The courts have also held that, whenever a husband transfers property to his wife the presumption of advancement applies and the onus of proving that no gift was intended would be on the husband. The reverse of this is not true. No such presumption arises when a wife transfers or puts a property in the name of the husband (GLR2 1974: 11).

In recent times, the reality is that most married women are gainfully employed in one way or the other and make tremendous contributions to household expenditure. The law must necessarily have a closer look at what accrues to such women in the marriage under the Marriage Ordinance and come out with legislative directives to enable them to claim their accruals disregarding the constraints imposed on such women under Customary Law. Such a legislative instrument must seek to spell out the property rights of spouses since more and more married women continue to make remarkable contributions to the household wealth which sometimes is neither documented nor quantified. This is necessary to erase the notion that the male spouse is always the great provider for the family. "Thus the question as to what interest accrues to a married woman who assists the husband in property must surely yield a different answer than that provided by the early writers and the courts a few years ago" (Kuenyehia 1988).

In all these, the intention of the spouses must play a decisive role. For example, if a child or wife assists a husband to carry out his duties at his station or a child or a wife advances money or building materials to the husband/ father for a house for the family, the intention of the wife or child must be established to differentiate this gesture from a mere assistance to the husband/father. Such differentiation are necessary to entitle the woman/child to at least their share in the house; the husband's share becomes devolved upon his family represented by his successors. If an evidence shows that the husband made an oral gift in his lifetime to either the wife or the child the whole property goes to the wife and children.

With regard to land ownership, both female and male stool subjects and lineage members had access to stool and lineage lands in the pre-colonial Ghana.

> In practice, however, this right did not operate on equal terms for both men and women. This is because in the early days, women tended to marry at very early ages and were thus soon encumbered with domestic chores and even more with the customary law obligation which required a woman to assist her husband with cultivation of his farms. It is to be noted that no corresponding customary law rule existed for men (Duncan 1997: 35).

On the farm, activities have been gender associated and there has been gender division of labour. The husband often undertakes heavier tasks of clearing the land, tilling, planting, and hunting while the wife assists with weeding in the cropped land, the cultivation of food crops, harvesting and collecting of foodstuffs and gathering firewood for everyday home use.

Other rights in customary marriage include the right by either the male or female to sue and be sued. The enforcement of the English law diminished the legal status of the Ghanaian woman in the colonial era. Marriage then meant a merger of identity of husband and wife. The woman could not own her own property. She could not sue her husband as before but she could be sued for offences like adultery or negligence of her duties as a wife. This meant that the traditional Ghanaian woman was a more liberal person than the modernized Ghanaian woman under the English law (Duncan 1997: 37).

Other factors that militated against the woman under this era were the commercialization of land for large-scale farming, sudden emergence of gender pattern of production—men produced cash crops and women produced food crops—which hitherto were only for subsistence and not for cash.

Colonial rule believed then that wealth and power were domains of men and only men. Female labour became neglected while favourable attention was paid to the growth of cash crops through the provision of extension services, research and technology. Since the food crop sector in which women were then involved did not receive these services, their production was marginalized.

Even though women were predominantly involved in cocoa (cash crop) production in the Akim area in the pre-colonial era, women were left out when companies were being formed for cocoa production for exports; women could not join companies in their own right. Married women could not, therefore, earn incomes from cash crop sales, they merely assisted their husbands in the production and sale of cash crops.

Women showed their inacceptance in various forms in different places during even the colonial rule. For example, the 1929 women's revolt in the Abo Region and the 1959 revolt in Eastern Nigeria were to seek redress to women's plight (Boserup 1970).

Also, it was discovered by the Watson Commission in Ghana in 1948 that the urban riots evolved from the shift from food crop development to cash crop development (Sarris et. al. 1991).

Under the colonial rule, land transactions became formalized throughout the country and land sales, mortgages, gifts and wills of land were effected by deed or in writing. These writings could be memoranda of disposition (in customary form) or dispositive acts involving English conveyancing precedents. Since women in this era did not have equal formal educational exposure with men, the latter form of document was to their disadvantage.

Rights in Divorce

Generally, either the woman or man can instigate a divorce. Among the Ewes, only the wife can instigate a divorce whereas in northern Ghana, it is the man that tradition allows to instigate a divorce.

Usually, husbands can seek divorce on grounds of adultery (but not vice versa) infertility, desertion or witchcraft. A wife can instigate a divorce on grounds of impotence, desertion, cruelty or neglect to maintain. (Duncan 1997: 112).

Divorce is effected through settlement between the two parties in the presence of family members from both sides and their legal representatives. Alimonies are given in settlement and are usually in the form of drinks and monetary compensation to the woman's family as in the Volta Region or in addition to the aforementioned, cloth and portions of the husband's farm or property can be given to the woman directly as in the Akan areas, Ashanti Region and Brong Ahafo Region.

In the Northern Region, however, a woman receives nothing upon divorce, not even the children and it is only at the discretion of the husband that she may be given something or even have access to the children (Duncan 1997: 113).

Danquah (1928) states that in Akim Abuakwa, the husband is entitled to half the profit of the work done by the wife.

> If, however, the wife would do some work for her own benefit, such as make cocoa farms, etc., on her own ancestral land, the husband has a right to half the property on divorce. So it is, if she trades. Should the husband, whether native or stranger, farm with her on ancestral land of his wife, he would be entitled to half share of such cocoa farm on divorce (Danquah 1928: 154).

Kuenyehia (1988) thinks the above statement is rather unclear and contradictory to what Customary Law holds.

> There is absolutely no reason why a husband should be given an interest in the wife's earnings and also to receive half the fruits of the wife's labour acquired without his help. At most, the husband's interest in the wife's private earnings should be limited to what is needed or used for common maintenance of the household.

Special legislative directives are necessary to give the due recognition to the fact that today, most married women engage in a gainful employment of a sort and make tremendous contributions to household expenses and such efforts must be duly compensated for when there occurs a divorce. For example, it was reported that "a divorced customary law wife successfully claimed one half of a cocoa farm jointly cultivated by the husband and herself on a piece of land belonging to her (Kuenyehia 1988)".

It has been observed that divorce settlements have been deliberately resisted by men. Divorce settlement has, over the years, been dependent on the woman's relationship with the man's family and on whether she is responsible for the break-up of the relationship. A woman does not receive alimony settlements if she instigated the divorce and men deliberately refuse or delay divorce proceedings in order to avoid alimony settlements. This notion is discriminatory against womanhood and sets out to blackmail a woman to continue to live with a man she may find violent or in any manner unacceptable (Duncan 1997: 113).

Upon dissolution of the marriage, either party submits bills for expenses incurred on the other's behalf during the marriage. The husband's bill could include the return of the bride price, advances for purposes of trade, debts paid on behalf of the wife and gifts of valuable trinkets. With regard to children, it depends on whether the divorce occurs in a patrilineal or matrilineal community. In the case of the former, the husband/father is given the absolute right to take full custody of the children whilst in the case of the latter, the wife/mother is granted custody of the children (Duncan 1997: 114).

Today, it may be worthwhile to have a legislative instrument that gives due consideration to the income levels of both parents. Thus, a woman may be granted custody even in a patrilineal community provided her income can sustain the children and vice versa. In northern Ghana, the rule on children is strictly observed and children as well as farmlands are for the men. Women feel very disadvantaged by this, for sometimes, the men shift the children on to relations and they do not receive the best of treatments. Women in northern Ghana, therefore, suffer and are deprived of their children as well as farmlands which are relevant resource for their lives.

Even though women in the Akan areas may have access to say 50 per cent of their farmlands as discussed earlier, Duncan (1997) suggests that "a unified system of divorce settlement (or alimony payments) be formulated and rendered applicable to all marriages whether under Customary Law or under the Ordinance".

Rights Concerning Marriage, Divorce and Property Ownership

Dissolution of marriages are effected by the courts, but generally most women do not like to resort to the courts to dissolve their marriages or make claims on inheritance from the courts.

The Courts Act., Act. 459 of 1993, gives the courts of Ghana jurisdiction to entertain divorce matters in the area of customary law divorce.

The Intestate Succession Law, 1985

From the earlier discussions, the family can be said to consist of all persons who are linealy descended from a common ancestor or ancestress and are deemed to share a common blood relation. By this definition, wives in all Ghanaian communities and children in matrilineal communities are not members of the husbands' or fathers' families respectively and until the passage of the Intestate Succession Law in 1985 (PNDC Law 111), were excluded from inheriting any shares in the estate of a deceased husband or father. At present, in the absence of a valid will, it is the PNDC Law 111 which guards property of couples, replaces and addresses the anomalies in the previous property laws.

This law applies to all class of people in all types of marriage in Ghana (Section 1 of PNDC Law 111,1985). It lays emphasis on the nuclear family (i.e. husband, wife and children) rather than the traditional family unit.

The Law has repealed Section 48 of the Marriage Ordinance which, among other things, gave a specific portion of the intestate's estate to the surviving spouse and Section 10 of the Mohammedan Ordinance which governed the distribution of the estate of a deceased spouse whose marriage was registered under the Ordinance.

As discussed earlier on, in Customary Law, each individual in the marriage retains and owns his/her property before and during the marriage. Children in matrilineal systems of such marriages have no claim other than maintenance offered by their father's successor and their right to live in their father's house was subject to their good behaviour and not by right.

The Intestate Succession Law, (PNDC Law 111,1985) sets out to consider the undermentioned point if a spouse dies intestate (without a will) or partially intestate with a will covering part of his/her property. It is based on moral justice.

It emphasizes that a surviving spouse be compensated for his or her services to the deceased spouse to enable the living spouse to cater more effectively for the children and gives recognition to even women surviving spouses who are also considered as part of the man's economic unit.

The provisions of succession under the Marriage Ordinance were discriminatory. A widower was entitled to more of the wife's property than a widow in respect of her husband's property.

The Intestate Succession Law now recognizes each partner in the marriage as a spouse and distribution is the same whether it is a surviving man or woman.

The property covered in this law includes only self-acquired property and not property held in trust by him/her for the community or a stool or as a family head. Essentially, this law addresses the following issues;

1. Application of the Law.
2. Intestacy and partial intestacy.
3. Devolution of household chattels (Section 18 of the Law).
4. Spouse or child or both to be entitled to one house.
5. Intestate survived by spouse and child.
6. Intestate survived by spouse only
7. Intestate survived by child only.
8. Intestate survived by parent only.
9. Devolution of residue where customary law is inapplicable.
10. Where customary law provides for succession by family.
11. Intestate survived by neither spouse, parent nor child.
12. Small estates.
13. Secretary may alter value of residue, etc.
14. Sharing of portion of residue by two or more persons
15. Presumption against survivorship.
16. Grand children of intestate.
17. Offence against an entitled person.
18. Interpretation.
19. Repeals.
20. Statutes and laws ceasing to apply.
21. Transitional provisions.

FIDA and other legal practitioners seriously enforce the Law and helped a lot of women out of the predicament of who owns what when a spouse dies intestate. Children covered under the Law are children who relate to the Intestate by status that is by the fact that they have been born to the particular intestate and not those children in the extended family who are children because they are of a limited chronological age of youth or infancy (Mensa-Bonsu and Dowuona-Hammond 1996). Thus, the child retains that status throughout his or her lifetime with its concomitant rights and duties. The child's rights include a name, residence, maintenance, testate succession, intestate succession, physical and moral protection, subjection to parental authority and the right to enter into contractual relations with adults.

Chapter 5

CONCLUDING REMARKS

Peculiarities of Motherhood

Motherhood is central to many women's lives. It shapes their relationship with other people. It makes and unmakes the woman; their opportunities for paid employment, their leisure activities and their individual identities. Why are some mothers satisfied and others not? What choices do mothers have and what are the consequences of these choices? The opportunities and constraints concerning motherhood will surely differ according to race and tribe, class, age, sexual life as well as the vagaries of the individual upbringing, we, as parents, received ourselves.

"Most mothers in industrial and non-industrial, urban and rural societies are oppressed." (Nicolson 1993: 203). Even though they have particular responsibilities they do not have the accompanying rights to choose how they mother or whether to mother at all. The resulting psychological effect on relationships between mothers and children has been passed on from generation to generation and mothers seem to be destined to disappoint themselves as well as their children.

Motherhood has both negative and positive experiences—the negative being the tiring, depressing experiences inherent in the social structure and the positive experiences being the exciting, rewarding and emotionally-stimulating satisfaction and fulfilling experiences offered by the children. Having children brings greater vitality, fun and humour into mothers' lives.

Motherhood is not a universal experience. It depends on the particular conditions—both social and economic—in which individual women give birth to or rear children. For example, having the help and support of a partner, family and friends or having enough money to be able to pay for someone to look after one's child are factors that are likely to make a significant difference to how a woman experiences motherhood. From a personal experience, Gertrude Mongella, an Assistant Secretary-General of the UN, thinks motherhood is only complete with fatherhood. Motherhood must be seen to complement fatherhood. The mother must play her part and the father his part. In appreciating the richness and significance of growing up in a small village in East Africa, she emphasized how being a mother is considered a blessing. She remarked how everybody around the expectant mother shows interest in the pregnant woman. When a woman is expecting, her father is expecting, her mother is expecting, her in-laws are expecting, her husband is expecting and the neighbours are expecting (Bourvard 1996: 230). This is what makes being a mother so pleasant in most African societies including Ghana. Mothers need and depend on social support.

If motherhood is to become a less-exhausting, onerous and costly experience for women, the work and responsibility of child-care needs to be shared effectively. The question is with whom? Over the years, men make little or very small contribution to the daily business of caring for children and continue to do very little of the unpaid job in the home. There is the need to massively change the attitudes and structure of society in the way and manner child-care and domestic work are organized to facilitate the needed support from men to ease the pressure on mothers in the homes.

However, in doing this we must not lose sight of the fact that we have to maintain the male role model or father figure to enhance the confidence of the child and ensure the normal healthy and psychological development. Shared parenting could work against the struggle for better public provision for child-care and we need to insist on public responsibility for child-care as we do for formal education for children after the age of five. Giving birth, as noted by Gertrude Mongella, can be either joyous or a bitter experience depending upon the availability of social and cultural support (Bouvard 1996).

What are some other changes or factors that are needed to make life easier for women as mothers? Women should be able to blend having children with having a job. In other words, women should be able to have children as working mothers and find the latter supportive of their motherhood roles rather than an alternative to their motherhood roles. Mothers need strength to cope with mothering and with its associated social conditions—child rearing, running the home, managing complementary childcare arrangements, maintaining relationship with their partners, family, friends and others. This strength will maintain a sense of their own identity and fulfil some of their own needs and help them find their way through the associated social subordination. This underlies the shift of national development approaches from the welfare approach to human resource development approach. The former approach held that women are solely passive recipients of development benefits because their major roles are reproductive ones — motherhood and childrearing whilst men's work is identified as productive. The latter approach, however, recognizes both the reproductive and productive roles of women and aims at creating better lives with greater freedom and well-being for members of the family, the local community and the society as a whole (Snyder and Tadesse 1995).

A very positive gain over the last two decades that promised better lives for women and girls is the girls' attendance at school in greater numbers and to higher levels. The momentum of that gain needs to be largely maintained and supported by government which will continue to encourage peasant families and low-income families to send their children to school. Such low-income families have had to choose between educating the boy in preference to the girl where payment of school fees is a limiting factor.

Even when girls are educated in hard time, jobs are not guaranteed. There is the need for political pressure if the gains made in formal education and its relation to employment are not to be reversed; that is leaving girls out of school to the home as their less-privileged uneducated lot.

Another point of consideration is that even though there is visible progress in the enrollment of girls from primary to tertiary levels, girls still lag behind boys in the critical contemporary fields of science and technology. Further, adult education programmes are to be intensified by the women organizations mentioned in this write up to educate women on their legal rights through inheritance affecting widows and divorced women and children and other types of ownership and/or usufruct rights to land. Violence against women is another area for legal literacy.

Women's empowerment is meaningless without economic independence. If evidence shows that most women spend all their income on their homes than men do, then an economic empowerment of the women will go a long way in making lives in the homes better — women can have a choice of ways by which to support themselves and their families. Women's empowerment seems to emanate automatically from their economic empowerment and independence and does not need to be agitated for any longer. Thus, the democratization process needs to be concerned about how to operationalize economic empowerment for women.

If women are to be economically empowered, international trade has to become a women's issue. There is the need to exchange experience and promote supportive policies for agriculture, agro-industry, other micro-enterprise and internal trade to enable women to support their families.

Enhancing women's access to other work related resources such as credit technologies, marketing and management advice and training is making an impact but more efforts need to be put in to effectively empower women and for that matter mothers economically.

Mebo Mwaniki, the newly appointed Chief of African Training and Research Centre for Women (ATRCW), a brain child of Economic Commission for Africa (ECA), holds that:

> One thing that is very crucial to the women of Africa is economic empowerment. We will give more attention to entrepreneurship, and promote women's intra-Africa trade. We would like women to move away from the informal sector to get into large production and marketing. Women are moving into private business: consulting firms, legal firms, import-export, construction and such others. They can go into electronics and engineering. They can make it (Snyder and Tadesse 1995: 185).

Basic imbalance between genders disturbs the balance in the environment in the same way as the imbalance in the individual invades the web of his/her life and affects all her relationships. Treating women as equals, putting them in the centre of their lives heals and can be a source of national well-being just as a true balance between the genders is the source of a harmonious culture (Bouvard 1996: 125).

This way, women do not get penalized to suffer negative effects of being financially dependent on men or state benefits. The powerlessness of women in society is often a direct reflection of women's lack of financial independence and women will only gain such independence when they are able to participate on equal terms with men in paid employment.

In this regard the establishment of day-care centres as being undertaken by the 31st Women's Movement in Ghana has been a very supportive notion. It offers women a safe place to keep their children while they go out to work for income.

Institutionalizing Attitudes and Concerns of Motherhood

In considering motherhood, it is clear that we need to examine not only the social and material conditions within which women give birth or raise children but also the beliefs and expectations that they hold about reproduction and child-bearing.

There are attitudes that have an impact on women's self-image. Men's perception of the role and status of women were also seen as fundamental obstacle that resulted in women being overlooked and ignored as developers.

The ingrown attitudes continually manifest as conservative mentality that become an accepted norm which is shared by many women and girls. This, has over the years, resulted in the passive acceptance of the limitations of their traditional roles and make them hesitate to new fields both in their family life and their chosen career.

Improvement of participation, grass-root solidarity, transformation of attitudes towards improved sustained productivity from family levels to career levels necessarily require institutional support at grass-root, regional and national levels. Activities of specialized institutions and organizations in existence such as Planned Parenthood Association of Ghana (PPAG), the Christian Mothers Association and Young Women's Christian Association (YWCA) need to be intensified to have the needed practical impact on the quality of children women are supported to bear.

These associations at the regional levels can design training schemes that create the awareness in women and transform their attitude on child-bearing and family lives as supportive of their roles in their chosen careers thus making full use of their human resource potentials for development.

The second type of institutions needed are those at the national level. In Ghana, the activities of the Commission for Children, the National Council for Women and Development (NCWD) and the 31st December Women's Movement are commendable. Such organizations, among other things, would develop and promote programmes that will integrate women in all sectors of national development and take legislative and other measures against taboos, attitudes and customs that militate against women as traced from birth to adolescent through to adulthood and motherhood particularly during the child-bearing stages.

The national programmes in turn need to be integrated into partnership programmes internationally towards a global solution for all women regardless of race or religion to enhance the social, political and economic emancipation of women. Through such programmes, mothers will receive advice and opinions that could help shape their beliefs and expectations in motherhood. It will contribute to an idealized view of motherhood and the family which continues to be part of the official rhetoric of politicians and policy-makers, cultural and religious norms of society. We need to challenge the tendency to glorify and romanticize the family and motherhood whilst ignoring the realities involved in caring for children.

Politicizing motherhood could help mothers exercise their choice about reproduction which is denied to women in most societies and also in the recognition of giving birth as a significant cultural, economic and social contribution to nations and the world. When we put motherhood in its proper social, religious, cultural and political perspective, we see clearly some of the neglected questions mothers have to give answers to, some of the contradictions, in thinking about reproduction and childbearing and hopefully show that, as women, we can gain more power and control over decisions about when and how sexual activity takes place and, related to this whether we do wish to have children and when.

Definitions of 'good' motherhood emphasize material sacrifice and the child-centred nature of society which frequently puts children's needs and rights before those of their mothers. Mothers' love for their children is as important for their mental health as vitamins and proteins are for good health (Nicolson 1993). This love needs to be available all the time. It must be offered unconditionally regardless of the mother's own needs and circumstances. Sometimes, whilst supplying the basic conditions for survival and maintenance of their children, mothers experience a decline in their own capacities to the extent that it results in a self-defined sense of being unfit for tasks demanding intellectual skills (Nicolson 1993: 206).

Native Americans such as Awiakta and the feminist philosopher, Sara Ruddick revealed that love and thought are deeply connected in the process of mothering and hold that even though mothers' lives are filled with conflict, mothers develop ways of dealing with conflict that are consistent with the goals of protecting and socializing their children (Bouvard 1996: xvii).

A real mother not only has a vision for her children but also wants to work for their future, ensuring them a life of peace, freedom and dignity. Women can expect to receive little public support or sympathy if they blame their dissatisfactions with motherhood on their children. The effects of this are likely to be, as before, that by individualizing their difficulties, women risk the consequences of feeling guilty and concealing their guilt.

It is possible for women to interpret what they do not like about their motherhood in a way that validates their frustration. However, in doing this, women need first to be able to acknowledge that far from being an isolated individualized experience, the way they feel is an understandable response to the way childcare is organized in the society. This way, their frustration should not be blamed on themselves or their children but on the conditions within the societal environment which sets out to distinguish between those aspects which contribute to dissatisfaction in motherhood and those aspects which are more likely to emphasize and focus on satisfactions in motherhood.

Some Lessons drawn from the Scriptures

Religious concepts have had very influential roles in various aspects of our lives and our attitudes as Ghanaians. This section, therefore, outlines a few encounters that women had in the scriptures to enable us to apply their experiences to our personal lives as mothers and as policymakers on matters that affect mothers as nation builders. Our Biblical lessons narrate vividly some of the encounters that some women went through with regard to marriage, motherhood, family and work.

Rebecca, the daughter of Bethuel, as a virgin had an encounter at the well when she met Abraham's servant asking her for a drink of water from her jar. She quenched his thirst when she offered him water from her jar and went further to offer water to his camel. Her favoured service earned her a gold ring which he fixed onto her nose and two large gold bracelets which were put on her arms (Genesis 24: 15-21). She ended up offering a place in her father's house to the servant. The servant was very pleased and offered praises to God for fulfilling His promises to him, for directing him to the woman he will win over to offer as a wife to Abraham's son. The servant appreciated the assistance of Laban, Rebecca's brother and at her consent offered clothing, silver and gold jewellery to her brother and mother. She received their blessing and agreed to join her betrothed through Abraham's servant. Then, Rebecca became Isaac's wife and filled in for the loss suffered from the loss of his mother, Sarah.

When Rebecca became pregnant, she experienced a lot of struggles in her womb and through prayers it was predicted to her that she was to be the mother of twins, apparently two rival nations, one stronger than the other, the older to serve the younger. Rebecca had a non-identical twins, a reddish and hairy Esau and the non-hairy Jacob (Genesis 25: 23-24).

Rebecca as mother exhibited differential love to her two sons. She assisted Jacob to receive his father's blessing which he meant for Esau. As a mother, robbing one son of his priviledge to pay the other could only be seen as the normal mothers love which, most invariably, is meant to offset a danger and to solve a problem.

Esther, a beautiful girl with a good figure was an adopted child of Mordecai. Her beauty won her an immediate favour in the King's royal palace amongst many other girls and she was assigned seven girls to serve her. On the advice of her foster father, Esther hid her identity as a Jew. After the regular massage treatments she and the many girls received,

Concluding Remarks

she won the favour and affection of King Xerxes and he gave her the royal crown and made her a queen. She reported a plot on the King's life and had the plotters executed and saved the King's life. By her courage and devotion she saved her Jewish race from being exterminated by their enemies (Esther 2: 15-23).

Elizabeth was the wife of the priest, Zechariah. Elizabeth was also from a priestly family. She and Zechariah led very good lives in God's sight but had no children together at an old age. Through prayers, Zechariah was blessed with the son, John. John's birth was predicted by the angel Gabriel to put things right, bringing fathers and children together again after a long separation, turning disobedience people to thinking righteously. Zechariah's disbelief was plagued with dumbness and this disgrace was undone when the angel's word was fulfilled through the pregnancy of Elizabeth and the birth of John. Elizabeth's pregnancy preceded that of Mary, the mother of Jesus. Elizabeth had a great joy and gladness when she was honoured with Mary's visit at the sixth month of her pregnancy. Elizabeth received a social support from Mary by this gesture and was so glad that even the baby within her was filled with gladness (Luke 1: 44).

Rachel was Laban's daughter and, therefore, Jacob's cousin (Rebecca was Jacob's mother and a sister of Laban). Rachel had a sister Leah, the first and elder daughter of Laban, all nieces to Rebecca.

Jacob fell in love with his cousin Rachel and was ready to work for his uncle, Laban to enable him to marry Rachel. However, Rachel's sister, Leah was the one Laban gave to Jacob at night and Jacob discovered this only after sexual relationship had occurred (Genesis 29: 15-26) Rachel had to lose her first place to her sister because it was not customary for the younger sister to be married before the elder one.

Even though Rachel, the loved one also became Jacob's wife she remained childless and Leah had children first. Leah had Reuben, Simeon, Levi and Judah. Rachel became jealous of the sister. She, Rachel, had to offer her maid to the husband Jacob so that she could mother his child. Her maid had two children for the husband which made Leah jealous and she, apart from her four sons, offered her maid to the husband and she also had two other sons.

Rachel's rival sister continued and had two more sons and a daughter, Dinah. It was only after Leah had enough that Rachel could start bearing children for Jacob as Jacob's first love. Joseph was then born to Rachel.

Rahab, a prostitute in the city of Jericho, in the land of Canaan, housed two Israelite spies who were in Jericho to survey the city. When the King heard of their presence and demanded them from Rahab, she refused to give them up. She covered them up, hid them and deceived the King instead that they had left the city. She did that believing that they were God's own people. She entered into agreement with them ensuring that she and her family, father, mother, brothers and sisters will be saved if she covered up their presence and they won the city of Jericho. The spies fulfilled their covenant with her as she did for them and by that all her people, even slaves, were saved and Rahab's descendants are many in Israel today. It was with faith that Rahab and her family were spared. Rahab became righteous with God through her kind gesture to the Israelite spies (Joshua 6: 22-23). This was an exhibition of faith and she received God's grace, her people were saved, they multiplied and filled the land of Israel.

The experiences of these women exhibit self denial, love, faith and self sacrifice needed for the achievement of their roles as women or mothers. What do we have to sacrifice to attain our set goals in motherhood? What kind of love do we need to exhibit and what form of sacrifice and self denial do we have to make? Which of our actions really falls in our motherhood? Do we have faith in God in strengthening us to go through motherhood?

Like the apostle Paul in his letter to the Phillippians, I wish to say

> Finally, my brothers and sisters, whatever things are true, whatever things are noble, whatever things are just, whatever things are pure, whatever things are lovely, whatever things are of good report, if there is any virtue and if there is anything praiseworthy meditate on these things (Philippians 4: 8).

BIBLIOGRAPHY

Ardayfio-Schandorf, E. (ed) 1994). *Family and Development in Ghana.* Accra: Ghana Universities Press.

Ardayfio-Schandorf, E. 1995. The Changing Family in Ghana: *Proceedings of the National Research Conference* held at the Golden Tulip Hotel Accra, Ghana, January 25th-27th, 1995, Accra: Friedrich Univerities Press.

Boserup, E. 1970. Women's Role in Economic Development In Women *in Agriculture in Ghana* quoted in B.A. Duncan. Accra: Friedrich Ebert Foundation, Ghana Office.

Bouvard, M. G. 1996. *Women Reshaping Human Rights: How Extraordinary Activists are Changing the World.* Scholarly Resources Inc.

Brown, C. K., N. A. Anokye and A. O. Britwum 1996a. Women in Public Life. Accra: Friedrich Ebert Foundation, Ghana Office.

Brown, C. K., N. K. T. Ghartey and E. T . Ekumah 1996b. *Women in Local Government.* Accra: Friedrich Ebert Foundation, Ghana Office.

Danquah, J. B. 1928. *Akan Lawa and Customs.* London:

de Graft Johnson, K.E. 1994. Family research: the Ghanaian situation. In (ed. E.Arydayfio-Schandorf) *Family and Development in Ghana.* Accra: Ghana Universities Press.

Dolphyne, F. A. 1991. *The Emancipation of Women: An African Perspective.* Accra: Ghana Universities Press.

Duncan, B. A. 1997. *Women in Agriculture.* Accra: Friedrich Ebert Foundation, Ghana Office.

Gaskell, J. 1992. *Gender Matters from School to work* London: Open University Press.

Ghartey, N. K. T. 1992. *The Training of Women for Managerial Capabilities in the Modern Economy of Ghana,* New Series Discussion Papers No25, Bradford: DPPC.

Hanmer, J.1993. Women and Reproduction In *Introducing Women Studies-Feminist Theory and Practice,*(Richardson, D. and V. Robinson, eds). London: Mcmillan Press Ltd, pp. 224-249

Jackson, Stevi 1993. Women and the Family. Richardson D. and V. Robinson, eds pp. 177-200.

Kishwar, M.1993. The Continuing Deficit of Women in India and the Impact of Amniocentesis.

Kuenyehia, A. 1998. Women and family law in Ghana. An Article written as a Visiting Research Fellow at the Law Faculty of the State University of Leiden, Netherlands.

Laws of the Gold Coast. Volume 111.

Maynard, M. 1993. Violence Towards Women. In (Richardson, D. and V. Robinson, eds). *op. cit.,* pp 99-122.

Mensa-Bonsu, and Dowuona-Hammond, 1995. The child within the Ghanaian family. In (Ardayfio-Schandorf, E. ed.) *The Changing Family in Ghana.* Accra: Ghana Universities Press.

Nicolson, P. 1993. Motherhood and women's lives. In (Richardson, D. and V. Robinson, eds). *op. cit.,* pp. 201-223.

Nikoi, G. 1998. *Gender and Development.* Ghana. (1993 Kwame Nkrumah Memorial Lectures), Accra: Ghana Universities Press/ UCC.

Nyavor, C.B. and Seddoh S. 1991. *Biology for Senior Secondary Schools.* Accra: Unimax Publishers Ltd. (in association with Mcmillan Publishers Ltd., London).

Offei, W.E. 1998. *Family Law in Ghana.* Accra: Sebewie Publishers.

Republic of Ghana and UNICEF 1990. *Children and Women of Ghana.* Accra:

Sarris *et. al. 1991. Ghana under Structural Adjustment: The Impact on Agriculture and the Rural Poor.* Rome: The International Fund for Agricultural Development.

Snyder M.C. and M. Tadesse 1995. *African Women and Development.* Witwatersrand University Press.

Stanhope, R and H. Jacob, 1995. The Child Growth Foundation. In *Turner Syndrome: A guide for patients and parents (series 8).*

Stanhope, R and V. Fry 1995. The Child Growth Foundation. *In Turner woman: A Patient Guide* (Series 9).

Witz, A. 1993. Women at work. (Richardson, D. and V. Robinson, eds) *op. cit.,* pp. 272-302.

INDEX

adolescent, 17
ante-natal care, 18–19
childcare, 20–21, 27
chromosomes, 2, 10
Commission for Children, 70
conception
    methods to enhance, 4–5
Contraception, 4
courtship, 12
Development and Women's Study (DAWS), 40
Divorce, 60–61
    settlements, 62–63
Dolphyne, Florence, 39, 46
education *see* girl-child
embryo, 7–8
family, 25–26
    women in, 28–30
fertility drugs, 9 *see also* conception
fertilization, 5–6, 9, 16
FIDA *see* International Federation of Women Lawyers
foetus
    sex determination, 2–3
gamete
    male, 2
    female, 2
Ghana Federation of Business and Professional Women (GFBPW), 39
girl-child
    formal education, 31–32, 33, 48, 68
Hormones, 6, 15
Husband
    role of, 24
    selecting, 24–25
International Federation of Women Lawyers (FIDA), 37, 47
Intestate Succession Law (PNDC Law 111), 63–65
life partners
    choice of, 22–23
Mankind
    origin of, 1
Marriage, 51–60
    customary law, 51, 52, 55–60
    Mohammedan Ordinance, 51, 52, 55
    Ordinance (cap 127), 51, 52–55, 58
mate-selection *see* life partners

menstrual cycle, 15–16
Mongella, Gertrude, 66, 67
Mwaniki, Mebo, 69
Natal care,
    ante-, 18–19
    post-, 19 *see also* child care
National Board for Small-Scale Industries (NBSSI), 50
National Council on Women and Development (NCWD), 37–38, 46, 47, 50, 70
personality, 10
placenta, 6–7, 9
polygyny, 55
puberty
    girls, 10–11
queenmothers, 46
rape *see* sexual abuse
reproductive system
    male and female, 13, 14, 15
Ruddick, Sara, 71
sexual abuse, 12–13
sexual harassment, 44
socialization, 27–28
Thirty-First December Women's Movement, 38, 47 50, 70
unbilical cord, 9
United Nations Development Fund for Women (UNIFEM), 42
United Nations Economic Commission for Africa (ECA), 36
United Nations International Women's Year (1975), 31
Women
    access to credit, 50
    access to law, 47–48
    empowerment, 68–69
    household headed by, 36–37
    in academia, 35
    in politics, 34
    in scriptures, 72–75
    job market and, 33, 34, 36
    participation in public life, 40–42, 45, 46, 47
    voilence against, 42–44
Women in Agriculture (WIA), 48
Women World Banking, 47, 50
Zygote, 5–6

www.ingramcontent.com/pod-product-compliance
Lightning Source LLC
Chambersburg PA
CBHW021135300426
44113CB00006B/436